Praise for *Activate You*

“In order to manage your ADHD, you must u ... SPECT imaging and reprogramming your brain with the strategies included in this book, you can optimize your ADHD even greater to live a more confident life.”

—Daniel G. Amen, MD, twelve-time *New York Times* bestselling author and founder of Amen Clinics

“In her innovative and helpful new book, *Activate Your ADHD Potential*, ADHD coach Brooke Schnittman helps adults with ADHD decrease frustration, improve their routines, and live with more satisfaction. Writing in a friendly, personal tone and sharing her own struggles and triumphs with ADHD along the way, Schnittman looks at the role disruptors play and how her 3C Activation method can help transform them into more productivity and effectiveness. The book is chock-full of accessible and thought-provoking exercises that readers can use immediately to make changes in their lives. I will be recommending this book to all of my clients!”

—Sharon Saline, PsyD, leading ADHD psychologist

“Great book, don’t procrastinate!”

—Edward M. Hallowell, MD, psychiatrist and world authority on ADHD

“In her book, *Activate Your ADHD Potential*, Brooke provides a comprehensive plan to move through the process of challenge to accomplishment with clear guidance, examples, and actions. Along the way, she helps individuals understand and manage the difficulties they have faced in the past with insight and compassion. You are in great hands taking Brooke’s approach to develop your personal pathway to success!”

—Cindy Goldrich, EdM, ADHD-CCSP, ADHD/executive function parent coach, coach trainer, and teacher trainer

“Brooke Schnittman isn’t just an ADHD coach—she’s an ADHD powerhouse! Combining the skills of a dedicated coach and the lived experiences of a self-advocate, this book offers lessons and tools that those of us with attention challenges can put to work in our daily lives. Brooke is a true authority on understanding the challenges and benefits of ADHD, and the information she shares is invaluable.”

—Harold “Hackie” Reitman, MD, author/neurodiversity advocate/founder, DifferentBrains.org

"*Activate Your ADHD Potential: A 12-Step Journey from Chaos to Confidence for Adults with ADHD* is an exceptional and empowering guide that every individual with ADHD should read. As one of Brooke's close colleagues, I have had the honor and privilege of experiencing her ADHD coaching for over five years. This text encompasses Brooke's warm and loving yet clear and direct presence throughout. Brooke's expertise shines through as she guides readers through each step, offering relatable anecdotes, evidence-based techniques, and actionable advice. The tone is supportive and nonjudgmental, fostering a sense of understanding and camaraderie between the reader and the author. In this book, Brooke brilliantly celebrates neurodiversity, encouraging readers to embrace their differences and use them as powerful tools for personal growth and success. By the end of this journey, readers will have gained a deep sense of self-awareness, honed their executive function skills, and cultivated a newfound confidence in managing their lives. I wholeheartedly recommend *Activate Your ADHD Potential* to anyone seeking to transform chaos into confidence, unlock their true potential, and embrace the strengths that come with ADHD. This book has the potential to make a meaningful impact on the lives of anyone with ADHD, empowering them to lead fulfilling and successful lives."

—Christina Seamster, PhD, area head of school, Fusion Academy

"One of the worst things you can do is accept your present circumstances as destiny. In *Activate Your ADHD Potential*, Brooke has done an outstanding job of helping people build the awareness of who they are, acquire the confidence to harness their unique gifts, and develop the self-belief to create a future much brighter than they could ever have imagined. Read this book and turn your challenge into your superpower."

—James Whittaker, 3x bestselling author, *Success Magazine* speaker, and leading authority on how to Win the Day®

"As the Director of People for a global well-being company, it was extremely important to make sure our employees had the BEST TOOLS and ADVICE to navigate working from home during a pandemic. Brooke helped implement and navigate the best work-from-home practices WHILE DEALING WITH A TON OF DISTRACTIONS. Brooke and 3C Activation were absolutely inspirational and motivational.

"I HIGHLY RECOMMEND Brooke's 3C Activation course!"

—Dan Steinberg, DOP of Chopra Global

ACTIVATE YOUR ADHD POTENTIAL

A 12-Step Journey from Chaos to Confidence for Adults with ADHD

Brooke Schnittman, MA, PCC, BCC

Printed in the United States.

Cover and book design by Asya Blue Design.
Graphics by Rhiannon Richards.
Author photo by Peter Wald Photography.

ISBN 979-8-9890233-0-1 Paperback
ISBN 979-8-9890233-1-8 Ebook

For undiagnosed B, my CWB, and the Clements family.

A MOMENT FOR TERMINOLOGY

In this book, attention deficit/hyperactivity disorder and the abbreviation ADHD are used when referring to all three types of ADHD, including hyperactive/impulsive type, inattentive type, and combined type.

Attention deficit disorder (ADD) was removed from the Diagnostic and Statistical Manual of Mental Disorders (DSM) in 1994, although some people still use it today.

Additionally, throughout the book, there are times I use the word "ADHDer" to refer to an individual with ADHD or, as some may say, "an ADHD person."

ADHDer is not a medical term and is not meant to discredit the correct terminology for ADHD. ADHDer is a term that is used often around the ADHD community and is not meant to be offensive.

CONTENTS

WHO IS THIS BOOK FOR?

This book is a guide containing anecdotal practices, professional stories, and personal experiences. There are many reasons for feeling as though you have not reached your potential as an individual with ADHD.

This book is for you if:

- You are an adult with ADHD or suspected ADHD who is ready to make a change in the status quo or chaos of their ADHD life.
- You are an adult looking to maximize your executive functions.
- You are seeking to help someone who has ADHD or is suspected to have ADHD, and they are ready to make a change.
- You have compared yourself to others or relied on others to figure out what's next for you.
- You have trouble with decision-making and feel you need to ask everyone for their opinion before making a decision. You might even ask Google or ChatGPT to find the best answer.
- You sometimes make impulsive decisions, or you wait too long and opportunities keep passing you by. This might leave you feeling

paralyzed, ashamed, and less than others.

- You are looking to create momentum in your life and build greater productivity and confidence than you've ever had before.
- You want to execute in a planned way.
- You want to take on bigger challenges.
- You are ready to finally reach your potential.
- You are ready to understand what prevents you from creating momentum.

Here are some reasons you might not experience the power of this book:

- You are looking for a quick fix without putting in any work.
- You have "tried everything" and you are just reading this book because someone "made you."
- You are looking for this book to replace the need for coaching.

FOREWORD

Living with ADHD can be wonderfully exciting, full of creativity, and incredibly frustrating all at the same time. You may start projects but be unable to complete them. You would like to stay focused but even the littlest noise outside your window stops your concentration. Perhaps you've come to expect failure and lost your confidence to take risks. While you want to do things differently and lean into your strengths, you may be overwhelmed and discouraged by the natural challenges that come with having an ADHD brain.

If you are wondering how to reduce frustration, change your habits, and live a more fulfilling life, then this empowering book is for you. Brooke Schnittman, ADHD coach and founder of Coaching With Brooke, has worked with adults living with ADHD for almost twenty years. Her background as a coach and an educator combined with her passion about ADHD add to her credentials as an expert in this field. She also speaks from experience: Brooke shares in the book that she and several family members live with ADHD. She bravely talks about her own challenges and shows how her tools have fostered her own personal growth

I first met Brooke a few years ago when she asked me to present at her ADHD EdCamp. I was impressed with her dynamic energy, her passion for helping people with ADHD, her innovative programs, and the breadth of her knowledge. Plus, she's funny, warm, and very smart. We became fast friends and connected colleagues. Brooke runs an impressive organization that offers coaching, webinars, handouts, and a terrific podcast. Not only do I love what she brings to world of ADHD, but I also see the tremendous value in how her philosophy and her methods continue to assist thousands of people just like you.

Brooke's practical and compassionate method to living more effectively, the

3C Activation© program, forms the foundation of this informative and useful book. The main theme centers around understanding and identifying those disruptions in our routines due to living with an ADHD brain. Then you learn to transform them and live with more productivity, satisfaction, and delight. These disruptors frequently result in a spiral of negative thinking and deep shame that prevent folks from building essential momentum, sticking with goal-oriented persistence, and nurturing healthy self-esteem. Brooke identifies a number of extremely useful techniques to add to your ADHD toolbox such as the 1% rule, mind mapping, the life cup, funnels, and many more. She also addresses how you can better care for yourself and develop healthier habits.

I especially like how Brooke takes complicated information about ADHD and breaks it down into understandable chunks. With many innovative exercises, forms, and reflections threaded throughout the book, you will feel like Brooke is sitting right next to you, assisting you in the process of change. Demonstrating her empathy and care, she teaches you to name and develop your character strengths to stop the downward spiral led by your disruptors. In addition, she offers you many ways to keep your momentum going after you finish the book by becoming involved with her community.

While you may think that you've tried everything, I don't think you've tried what this book has to give you. Take the plunge and see how your life can shift positively. As Brooke says, start small. Very small. By reading this, actually, you are already on your way. I sincerely believe that *Activate Your ADHD Potential* will help you change your life for the better.

—Sharon Saline, PsyD, author of *What Your ADHD Child Wishes You Knew: Working Together to Empower Kids for Success in School and Life* and *The ADHD Solution Deck*
drsharonsaline.com

CHAPTER SUMMARIES

Chapter 1: How to Operate this Book with ADHD ... For Those Who Find Directions Disruptive

This opening chapter provides basic directions on what you can expect from this book. Because directions are disruptive and not everyone is at the same step in life, this chapter directs you on where you may want to start your journey through this book.

Chapter 2: What Is Momentum and How Does It Work?

The first step is to understand what momentum is and why it's important. It is not an area where ADHDers generally excel. We typically have an all-or-nothing mindset and have high intensity for periods of time on things that interest us. It is extremely difficult to build and keep momentum.

Chapter 3: The Ten Ways ADHD Can Disrupt Momentum

In this chapter we will discuss the path that disrupts momentum for individuals with ADHD, leading to overwhelm or underwhelm, both of which are extremely disruptive and leave us with a lot of shame and negative self-beliefs. In order to stop this spiral, we need to understand what stands in our way and gain awareness. I have listed the ten ways below. We will go into each one and what they are in greater depth in chapter two, so you don't feel alone when you are at this place in your ADHD spiral.

The ten disruptors are:

1. Underwhelm
2. Exciting New Idea/Dopamine Rush
3. Hyperfocus
4. Overwhelm
5. Burnout
6. Low Dopamine
7. Emotional Dysregulation
8. Feelings of Failure/RSD
9. Comparison/RSD
10. Shut Down

Chapter 4: CWB's 12-Step Journey for Building Momentum

How do you escape overwhelm or underwhelm (or anywhere between) and STOP the continuous spiral? I have laid out twelve tools below. These are meant to be reviewed in order. The first steps show us how our brain works and how to maximize its usage. In the next steps, we learn to maximize our time and become confident. Take as much time as you need. Do one topic per day, week, or even month to get what you need. I also highly recommend you enlist a buddy (friend, significant other, coach, mentor, trainer) while you are going through this to hold yourself accountable.

1. 1%
2. Mind Map
3. Life Cups
4. Values
5. Strengths
6. Figure Out Why
7. Make them SMART
8. Dopamine
9. Organization
10. Procrastination
11. STOP the Stress
12. Next-Level Requests to Feel Empowered

Chapter 5: I Have Built Momentum! Now What?

In this section, we present potential paths to continue your personal development journey. Please review this chapter after going through the previous chapters.

Chapter 6: The Secret Support System That Maintains Momentum.

This section helps you to understand what you might need AFTER reviewing the strategies in chapter four. (You were taught this as a kid, but everyone overlooked it then.) It is important to complete the key steps before taking on this section.

Chapter 7: Client Experiences with CWB's 12-Step Journey—This Really Works!

For privacy, the names in this chapter were changed. Every client in this chapter came to Coaching With Brooke due to overwhelm or underwhelm. We worked on CWB's 12-Step Journey for Building Momentum that we discussed in chapter four. Each client was of a different age range and had different experiences throughout the 12-Step Journey for Building Momentum. Some left with their goals unmet but discovered new insights that changed their life, some met their goals soon, and some took months to build traction and awareness. The key in going through this chapter is to understand that no two journeys are the same. We all have feelings of disruption as discussed in chapter three, and we can see an increase in positive momentum and confidence at different times of our coaching journey.

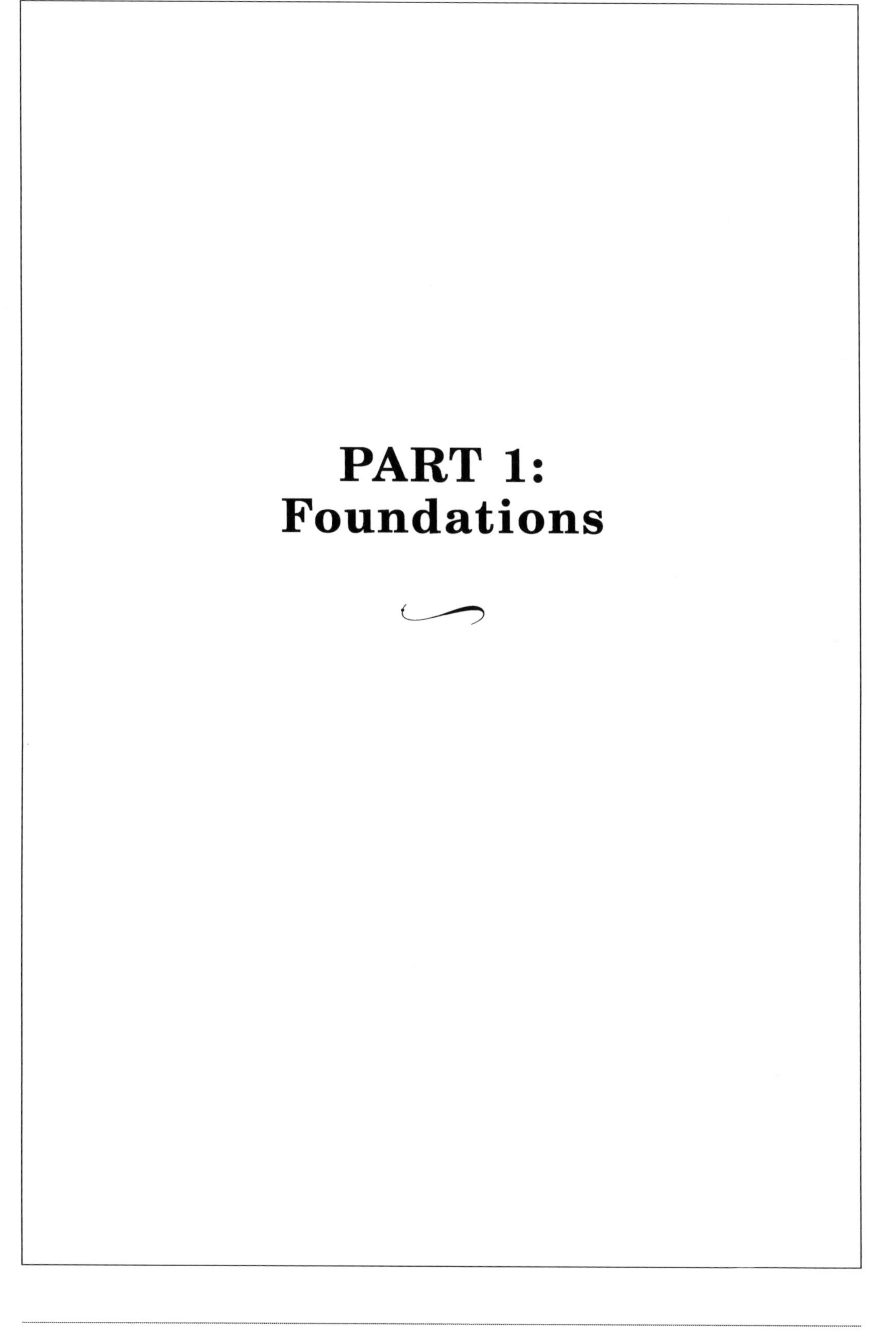

PART 1: Foundations

CHAPTER 1

How to Operate this Book with ADHD ... For Those Who Find Directions Disruptive

As an ADHD coach, I want to guide you by sharing my experiences. Since 1998, I have worked alongside individuals with ADHD. In 2006, I began professional work with ADHDers and have devoted my life to helping them and their families. I have ADHD. My husband has ADHD. My two stepchildren have ADHD. My toddler displays ADHD symptoms (although she is too young to diagnose).

If you have ADHD, let's face three possibilities about you and this book:

1. You might have started reading this book in a different chapter.

2. You may not read the entire book and finish all of the lessons.

3. You likely will not read all the directions.

I completely get you! There is no shame if any of those three possibilities become a reality. I respect and honor the way you read and operate. Knowing that everyone won't read every word of this book, I have created a summary guide to help you on your momentum-building journey.

And if you can have a momentum-building journey, you will have the power in you to finish all of the lessons! You might not believe that right now, but I do. As a coach, I have seen the unbelievable transformation from the tried-and-true exercises in this workbook!

COACHING ENCOURAGEMENT

Check out the questions below. They will save you a lot of time!

Answer these questions.

Question #1: Do you understand the ADHD concept of momentum and what it looks like in your life?

Yes: Then go to question two.
No: Then you might want to start at chapter two.

Question #2: Are you able to identify the ten ways that ADHD can disrupt your momentum?

Yes: Then you may want to start in chapter four and begin implementing CWB's 12-Step Journey for Building Momentum.
No: Then you might want to start at chapter three.

I highly recommend you get an accountability partner as you work through this book. This can be a friend, significant other, family member, or even someone from the Coaching With Brooke Body Doubling Community.

If you have purchased this book, please go to > *bit.ly/CWBDiscord* to join our private Body Doubling Community. Body doubling can also be called co-working. It is helpful for individuals with ADHD to get tasks done. A body double is simply a person or pet that keeps you company while you tackle a task. It can be done virtually, on a voice call, or in person. They can just sit with you or complete their own task alongside you. You can watch a video on how the Body Doubling Community works by going to > *bit.ly/CWBDiscordHowTo.*

Having someone for accountability can help us to avoid jumping from task to task or getting distracted. It can be helpful to have extra hands or minds for big projects, too. If you don't have someone to body double with, you can also go to work on your task at a café, park, or library—anywhere other people hang out and where you can do work.

Body doubling can help you complete any task where you need extra motivation and initiative. This can include paperwork, homework, studying, working out, chores, and even eating. Feel free to learn more at > *bit.ly/POPBODYDOUBLE* from Coaching With Brooke alumni and lifelong body doubler, Marissa.

"In an individual sport, yes, you have to win titles. Baseball's different. But basketball, hockey? One person can control the tempo of a game, can completely alter the momentum of a series. There's a lot of great individual talent."

—Kobe Bryant

CHAPTER 2

What Is Momentum and How Does It Work?

What does the word momentum make you think about?

Is it a good association or a bad association?

First Example

Momentum might lead you to think of physics class in middle school or high school. You might recall that "momentum = mass times velocity" and that momentum is a measure of motion in an object.

That last paragraph might trigger negative associations. Maybe your ADHD caused you to struggle with classwork. Maybe other students appeared to have *momentum* and their life was always in motion and moving forward, while you were stuck and struggling to complete the problems and labs.

Second Example

You might associate *momentum* with sports. When you watch the NFL or NBA, you see many momentum shifts within games. The New York Giants might be down twenty to zero and then score two straight touchdowns to cut the lead. You would likely hear the sports announcer say, "Momentum is on the Giants' side." Perhaps you feel like the team who is on the wrong side of the momentum and giving away the lead. I believe this book will help you develop strategies to keep momentum moving in a positive direction.

Third Example

Now picture a grandfather clock. Picture how tall it is. Picture the walnut wood. Picture the glass. Maybe you see your reflection in the glass. Picture the numbers on the face of the clock. They are probably roman numerals. Picture the brass pendulum swinging back and forth.

Now hear the *tick-tock* of the pendulum. This is a type of momentum. Can you picture yourself sitting at a table in that room? You are working on your favorite hobby. The rhythm of the *tick-tock* soothes you and even helps you focus on your hobby. You are absorbed in your craft while the grandfather clock sets the tempo.

Then you hear a crash. The pendulum broke off from the clock. The *tick-tock* is gone. The rhythm is gone. Your groove is broken. Your work is disrupted.

Momentum and ADHD

The biggest challenge for ADHDers is handling disruptions in our daily routines that often result in a dysfunctional cycle of progress.

This vicious cycle presents us with many challenges:

- How do we begin a task?
- How do we finish a task?
- How do we keep our energy consistent?
- How do we stop the disruption cycle and get back to momentum?
- How do we not identify or define ourselves by this disruption?

If we don't break the cycle, we will default to one of two dreaded extremes: underwhelm or overwhelm.

To break this disruptive loop, we must first understand why it exists (chapter three) and what proactive steps will prevent disruptive behavior associated with suffering from ADHD (chapters four through six).

"Sometimes thinking too much can destroy your momentum."

—Tom Watson

CHAPTER 3

The Ten Ways ADHD Can Disrupt Momentum

Something stands in the way of you becoming confident, successful, and persistent. I call them Momentum Disruptors.

These ten disruptors can be experienced at any point throughout your day and journey. What triggers these disruptions? Your mindset, energy level, nutrition, sleep, life circumstances, lack of boundaries, lack of confidence, past history, lack of awareness, and lack of dopamine and tools feed the disruptions.

In this chapter, we will review the ten disruptors that prevent building and maintaining momentum. As we go through them, notice how each disruptor can flow into the next disruptor.

THE ADHD DISRUPTION SPIRAL

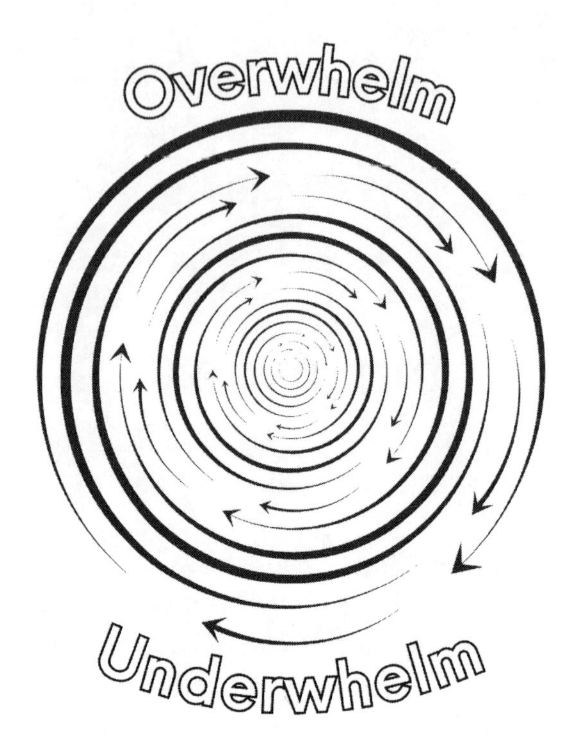

COACHING ENCOURAGEMENT

If you have gotten to this part of the book, the odds are that you have felt these ten disruptors at some point in your life, if not on a daily basis. To learn how to calm the chaos of your ADHD, start with the chaos. It is important to start with the awareness of what is getting in the way of building and maintaining momentum and ultimately feeling lifelong confidence.

Below are the ten ADHD disruptors we will be reviewing in this chapter.

1. Underwhelm
2. Exciting New Idea/Dopamine Rush

3. Hyperfocus
4. Overwhelm
5. Burnout
6. Low Dopamine
7. Emotional Dysregulation
8. Feelings of Failure/RSD
9. Comparison/RSD
10. Shut Down

Disruptor #1: WE ARE UNDERWHELMED

Are you ever paralyzed when facing challenges and scenarios where expectations are not put in place?

Do you ever lack the confidence to tackle a difficult task because you believe your past failures will not allow you to make meaningful contributions to current projects or ideas?

Do you ever struggle to take initiative with work tasks, household chores, or relationships?

Each of these can be symptoms of underwhelm. They are keeping you from reaching your full potential.

Underwhelm can set in when life is monotonous and you lack challenging tasks and accomplishments. Ironically, it also can set in when you are successful.

When we are not intrinsically motivated or excited about the task, we can hypofocus. Hypofocus was first discussed by psychologist Jordan Cohen. He described it as "a state of mind that inhibits concentration and distracts one's attention." It affects focus to the point where you have difficulty with energy or properly completing tasks. When we are hypofocused, we have low interest and are very often bored.

It is paralyzing to start on tasks that are uninteresting because low interest very often leads to low dopamine, which then leads to a lack of initiation.

Where else does the task paralysis and analysis paralysis of underwhelm come from?

- The inability to recover from a previous failure leading to momentum disruption
- Not truly knowing yourself because you have not identified nor live in your values and strengths
- Time management difficulties
- Executive dysfunction (a disruption in the ability to manage thoughts, emotions, and actions) impacting your ability to initiate

Underwhelm deeply impacts your sense of self and your abilities to adapt and explore new paths in life. Later in the book we will discuss ways to overcome underwhelm.

Surrounding ourselves with uninspiring people and activities could also add to the underwhelm as well.

Disruptor #2: EXCITING NEW IDEA OR OPPORTUNITY/DOPAMINE RUSH

Due to underwhelm, your brain can constantly be seeking the next new idea or opportunity. On the subconscious level, your brain is on alert for something exciting in order to increase its dopamine levels. Your excitement leads to dopamine surges.

ADHDers are known for their active imaginations and their enthusiasm for something new. This can help break you out of underwhelm. A big idea or grandiose opportunity generates excitement. Success seems tangible! You jump headfirst into a big, new venture.

You possess potential energy and momentum because you are constantly on the hunt for the next great challenge, whether it's a recreational goal or finding fresh answers to complex problems.

Why does that mental rush happen? Dopamine spikes lead to hyperfocus, and you can forget that everything else exists.

Disruptor #3: HYPERFOCUS

The surge of dopamine can lead you to hyperfocus on a new and exciting idea or opportunity. You jump into action to earn specific rewards and feel pleasure.

What is hyperfocus?

Have you ever become so engrossed in a task that you felt like your life could not have any other purpose than completing that task? Your excitement leads to tunnel vision, and, honestly, it can be an obstacle to productivity. This is what we call hyperfocus.

When you are in hyperfocus, your concentration on a particular task leads you to block out any distractions. Others might think you've left behind the world around you. Your brain *has* left the world around you.

Hyperfocus is the brain's way of intently focusing on something and disregarding all distractions. To complete writing this book, I needed hyperfocus sessions to pump out content. My clients have told me that when in a state of hyperfocus, they don't hear people talking to them. In that state, nothing else exists besides the task at hand. They skip bathroom breaks, food, water, and appointments.

Hyperfocus is connected to passion. If you weren't passionate about the new venture, then you wouldn't be fixated on it. The passionate endeavor is fueled by novel and liberating thoughts and ideas. You had not previously encountered such thoughts, and their seduction keeps you in this heightened state. In this trance state, your mind moves with greater speed and higher confidence through its current exploration.

Hyperfocus blurs boundaries between your tasks and disciplines. Exciting new concepts form! Hyperfocus can transform the fog of concentration deficiency into a beacon for sustaining effort and creating dramatic breakthroughs in your endeavors. Hyperfocus is not ALWAYS a disruptor, but it needs to be used in appropriate ways.

Disruptor #4: OVERWHELM

Hyperfocus can be a double-edged sword. One edge is that you accomplish a lot. The other edge is that you can become overwhelmed.

What is overwhelm?

It's like an artist who looks at a painting and believes it will never be completed. You can suddenly feel that your hyperfocus project will never be completed because you are incapable of completing it.

You will suddenly notice all the matters you ignored and realize that you have neglected many things and rush to get them all done. There might be consequences if you forget that appointment or forget to pay that bill. You might take on more tasks than you can manage and become consumed by all the things that need to be done. Workloads can quickly spiral out of control, leading to an overabundance of stress and anxiety.

Hyperfocus can force regular shifts between different activities or tasks in order to make progress. Completing tasks too quickly can lead to setbacks due to subpar work and lack of reflection once the task is completed. This can then lead to quality issues or technically incorrect assumptions or implementations.

Hyperfocus is a tremendous power to direct our thoughts and activities at impressive paces. However, when hyperfocus is mishandled, you can feel overwhelmed.

Disruptor #5: BURNOUT

On his website (*drhallowell.com*) American psychiatrist, worldwide speaker, and *New York Times* bestselling author Edward M. Hallowell, MD, explains that individuals with ADHD have a "Ferrari brain and bicycle brakes." You can push yourself to the limit when your dopamine is high and when you are in a state of hyperfocus. This leaves you with a massive depletion of dopamine, and it can be tough to rebound.

Dr. Hallowell says that individuals with ADHD are in a state of "now or not now." Check out his endorsement of the strategies in this book on his podcast episode of *SuccessFULL With ADHD*.

You can set extremely high standards when it comes to your goals. As a result, your aspirations sharply entwine around your mind in a way that, for many, appears nearly impossible to navigate their own paths. Research has shown this is due to how the ADHD brain unconsciously and continuously grasps for mental stimulation at more complex levels. This longing for challenging intellectual stimulation may inadvertently impede basic tasks such as completing achievable short- and long-term goals.

Setting lofty goals is a common trait among ADHDers. To those without ADHD, these goals can appear confusing and baffling. They are concerned for their loved ones as they wonder how any clarity and resolution will ever come from such chaos.

Your roadmap is not linear. That is hard for others to understand. To them, your roadmap may seem inefficient. ADHDers are driven by ambition and are firmly grounded in the passion that leads them to create intricate routes with multiple paths toward their destinations. This desire lays out plans that can seem willowy to outsiders. Yet when linked together, they make up a sturdy roadmap toward meeting your ambitions.

As goals become enormous, the pursuit of them becomes more complicated. You might start to think about old challenges and failures. You might get burned out.

Burnout can appear as fatigue (emotional, mental, and physical) and diminished motivation. Do you ever feel overwhelmed? Do you ever feel drained? Burnout is a mixture of those two. Burnout makes you feel unable to cope with the wide range of tasks and sources of stress in your life.

The most common cause of burnout is a prolonged period of intense stress mixed with an overwhelming mental workload. Are you taking on more than you can handle? Are you working at an unsustainable pace? If this is you and you have unmanaged hyperfocus, you are in danger of burnout.

What else causes burnout?

- Repetitive tasks
- Unclear role expectations
- Prioritizing productivity over rest
- Competing demands from multiple people in our lives
- Toxic workplace environments

Disruptor #6: LOW DOPAMINE

Scientists have discovered that dopamine levels are different in people with ADHD than in those without it. ADHD was the first disorder discovered to be caused by the result of a deficiency of a specific neurotransmitter. ADHDers are deficient in norepinephrine.

ADHD was also the first disorder found to respond to medications to correct this underlying deficiency of dopamine. Like all neurotransmitters, norepinephrine is synthesized within the brain. The basic building block of each norepinephrine molecule is dopa. Dopa is converted into dopamine, and dopamine is then converted into norepinephrine.

You face the difficult task of understanding how and when your dopamine levels are optimal so you can stay focused on tasks and complete them. When dopamine signaling is impaired in your brain, this dysregulation often results in you struggling with tasks that seem mundane to others.

Your dopamine levels often influence your concentration, lack of impulse control, and restlessness. One of the challenges of managing your ADHD is managing your dopamine levels. Too little dopamine means that you can have difficulty controlling your emotions.

Disruptor #7: EMOTIONAL DYSREGULATION

ADHDers can have difficulty regulating their emotions because they have difficulty with their executive functions. We struggle with emotional regulation because we have not learned the proper tools.

Thomas E. Brown is a clinical psychologist who received his PhD from Yale University and specializes in the assessment and treatment of high-IQ children, adolescents, and adults with ADHD and related problems. He has forty years of experience and has contributed to over thirty journal publications, written seven books, and presented his work in almost fifty countries. He was inducted into the CHADD Hall of Fame for outstanding contributions to research and professional education about ADHD in children and adults. Dr. Brown has also been elected a Fellow of the American Psychological Association.

Different doctors and ADHD specialists have varying opinions on how to model executive functions. Dr. Brown categorizes our executive functions into six different "clusters" as shown in the diagram here: Activation, Focus, Effort, Emotion, Memory, and Action.

Each of these clusters is then broken down into subclusters.

Executive Functions Impaired in ADHD

Executive Functions
(Work together in various combinations)

Organizing, prioritizing, & activating to work
1 Activation

Focusing, sustaining, & shifting attention to task
2 Focus

Regulating alertness, sustaining effort, & processing speed
3 Effort

Managing frustration & modulating emotions
4 Emotion

Utilizing working memory & accessing recall
5 Memory

Monitoring & self-regulating action
6 Action

- Activation: Organizing, prioritizing, and activating tasks
- Focus: Focusing, sustaining, and shifting attention to the task

- Effort: Regulating alertness, sustaining effort, and processing speed
- Emotion: Managing frustration and modulating emotions
- Memory: Utilizing working memory and accessing recall
- Action: Monitoring and self-regulating action

According to Dr. Brown, these clusters work together, and individuals with ADHD struggle in all of the clusters in some way.

At its core, emotional regulation is about managing and directing feelings. It's not about ignoring, suppressing, or avoiding feelings. Emotional regulation is about understanding what those feelings mean and how to use them in making well-thought-out decisions. This is where executive functions come into play. Studies consistently show that the parts of our brain responsible for executive functions (such as planning, self-control, reasoning, and problem-solving) also help to modulate our emotions. Individuals with ADHD have a deficit in their executive functions, and this can lead to difficulty managing our emotions.

Disruptor #8: FEELINGS OF FAILURE/RSD

Due to items one through seven in The ADHD Disruption Spiral, individuals with ADHD can start to identify as a failure and have difficulty separating themselves as a failure from the failed task. This is common with rejection sensitive dysphoria (RSD). William Dodson, MD, explains that RSD can feel like physical pain in your chest. The emotional piece of RSD impacts ADHDers more than those without ADHD. Dr. Dodson said, "RSD is extreme emotional sensitivity and pain triggered by the perception that a person has been rejected or criticized by important people in their life. It may also be triggered by a sense of falling short, failing to meet their own high standards or others' expectations."

Although RSD is not in the DSM-5 (the classification system of mental disorders used by mental health professionals in the United States), this dysphoria has been experienced by a large number of my clients and other ADHDers worldwide.

Disruptor #9: COMPARISON/RSD

COACHING ENCOURAGEMENT

You might be comparing yourself right now to other individuals (neurotypical or not) by saying, "Why haven't I managed my ADHD yet?" Keep going! You are one step closer to managing your ADHD for life.

We compare ourselves to what we see others doing. This leads us to start working on another goal or task though we are lacking confidence. When you feel like a failure and lack dopamine, you can create stories that others are doing "it" better than you.

When writing this book, I went through all ten steps of The ADHD Disruption Spiral. I was very close to calling it quits on writing this book. I cast the idea of "The ADHD Disruption Spiral" for a TEDx talk in South Florida. I never heard back.

I spiraled into my negative thoughts. They sounded like this:

- "Why would anyone want to read this?"
- "ADHDers already know this."
- "Is this *REALLY* good enough for a book?"
- "Established authors have better stories to tell."
- "If TEDx hasn't replied back, this obviously is not important enough."

I felt like I wasn't as good as other people. I felt like I couldn't compete. I would think, "Why bother if I can't do it like someone else?"

Disruptor #10: SHUT DOWN

When feelings of failure eventually become *too much*, you will shut down completely. Your body needs to take a break from the overwhelming demands placed on it.

MOVING FORWARD

When I talked about the comparison disruptor, I told the story of writing this book. I was fortunate to catch myself before completely shutting down. I was able to catch myself because I realized I was going through the motions of The ADHD Disruption Spiral. I made comparisons. I was having RSD moments.

By using my ADHD toolbox, I was able to literally stop, pause, and come back to writing when I was in a better state of mind. This helped me drop my negative thoughts, my overwhelm, and my negative self-beliefs. The only deadline I had to write this book was the one I created for myself.

When I was calm, I came back to my writing because I realized that if I find this important, then others will too. If this process has already helped thousands of people, hopefully it can help millions of people with ADHD. I thought about how I have wanted to create my own podcast for five years. With the right support and tools, I have launched *SuccessFULL With ADHD*, and it is impacting ADHDers because in its first month of release, it was in the top 2.5% of all podcasts.

I also realized that I was dealing with a lot—a new baby and a fast-growing business. I had to ask myself, "Why am I putting so much pressure on myself?" Sound familiar?

As you go forward in this book, you will learn how to maintain your momentum. My goal was to write this book. Your goal is different, but you can achieve it, if you follow the steps to maintain momentum.

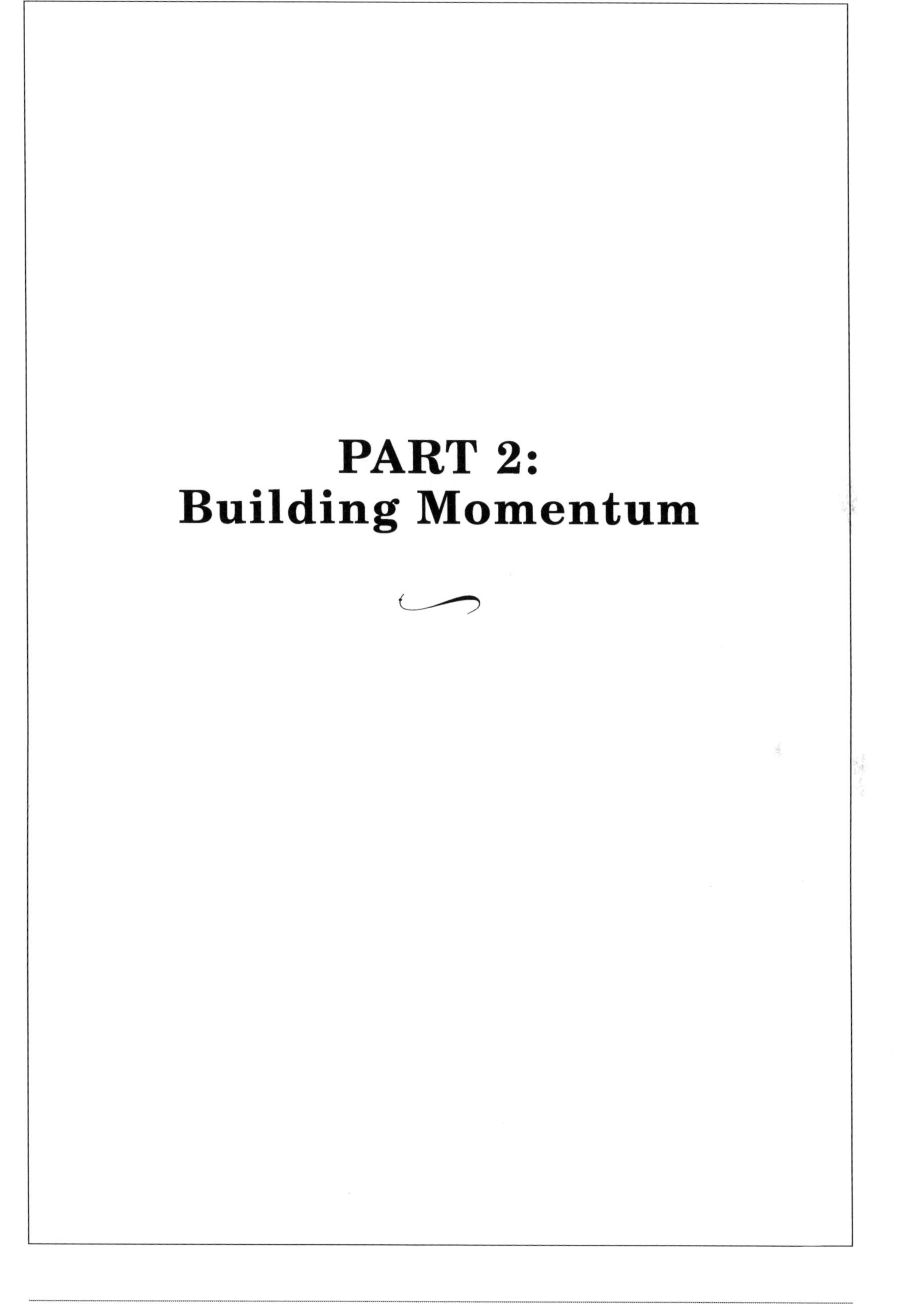

PART 2:
Building Momentum

“Momentum solves eighty percent of your problems.”

—John C. Maxwell

CHAPTER 4

CWB's 12-Step Journey for Building Momentum

If you want to build momentum, you have to first clear the chaos! In the last chapter, we discussed Momentum Disruptors. In this chapter, we will discuss strategies that have helped ADHDers gain momentum.

Emotional dysregulation that stems from ADHD can very often lead to chaos! You need to clear the emotional, physical, and mental chaos. Throughout childhood and perhaps into college, your parents and teachers acted as the executive functions of your brain. They inadvertently helped you create structures and routines, organize schedules and spaces, and plan events and a future. They often came to your rescue when you forgot something or messed up.

When I was in fifth grade, I had to give a presentation in class. The morning of the presentation, I was still putting handouts together. I still hadn't even printed them. I needed my mom to help me out because I missed some of the key details that were necessary for my presentation. I desperately needed my mom to act as my executive function, my safety net, and my protector. I needed her to make sure that I didn't fail or forget important details.

She would still act as my executive function as a young adult. When I was auditioning for a teaching role, I had to give a demonstration lesson on genetics. I obsessed over creating the perfect demonstration. I ended up hyperfocusing and going down rabbit holes. The presentation made no sense. The night before my presentation, I broke down. I was hysterical.

My mom came to the rescue. She was also in the teaching profession, and she connected me to one of her colleagues who talked me through what I should do for the presentation. I woke up confident the next day.

After a day of more bad decisions, I did get the teaching position.

Do you know why I called my mom? I felt I needed her help just like I did when I was in school. She called one of her teacher friends to help me break through my despair.

Once you arrive at adulthood, you very likely have not created systems and tools to manage your executive dysfunctions. You then live day-to-day without the ability to look peripherally into what's going on. You don't know how to see ahead.

Day after day this chaos builds up. You don't set clear boundaries. You say "yes" to too many things. There is no planning ahead. You don't know yourself, your strengths, your weaknesses, or what is important to you.

Chaos seeps into your pores. You sweat out utter frustration and shame.

Many of my ADHD clients have discovered that gaining the tools and confidence to build and maintain momentum is the key to success.

Think back to the executive function deficiency we just talked about. How did I ever overcome having breakdowns over forgetting to make copies for my presentation?

As an ADHDer, I had to strengthen my executive functions.

How did I do that?

In this chapter, we will discuss twelve strategies that thousands of ADHD clients and I have used to strengthen our executive functions. The key here is to start *small.* Think *smaller than you think is small.*

You can learn to build on your actions through completion. You might read some of this and say, "I've already heard this idea!" It is important to try it and incorporate these strategies in order.

For each strategy, you will see ***Your Turn >>*** throughout this chapter. There you will find an opportunity to work through these strategies.

This chapter is designed for you to work through and strengthen your executive functions. You may answer these questions out loud to yourself. You might prefer to write down the answers in this book, on a computer, or on a device. Do what works best for you and your learning style.

COACHING ENCOURAGEMENT

Most of my clients do best when they write the answers with pen and paper. It improves their working memory for each task and increases their chance of completing the task.

And remember: do the tasks in order. Give yourself some time between each step. I recommend approximately one week between each step because I have found this is enough time to take action on your current step.

Here's What to Expect from These Strategies

In order to slow and stop the chaos, you need to start with the chaos. This means shining a light on the parts of your life that are unbalanced. You will learn the subconscious beliefs that have blocked you from living in alignment with your actual strengths and values. No more beating yourself up for the mistakes you've made or replaying failures in your head.

You will learn to use cutting-edge methodologies that will allow you to discover and embrace what makes you uniquely you. You can overcome questioning yourself and feeling shame. The initial sense of encouragement and "I can do this!" will likely surface during this process. You'll be filled with excitement as new possibilities emerge and we design your unique plan of action.

Once you've uncovered the crucial blocks that have been in your way for years, you will next test what you've learned with new, and likely uncomfortable, actions. You will learn paths to action for your unique and specific goals as you develop your WHYs and WHATs.

You will use the proven framework from *How to Focus by Focusing Your Time: 13 Ways to Be Productive*. You'll be equipped with the tools and support you need to stay focused, even on the most challenging days. You might say, "I've tried that before!" Do you know what will be different this time? You will learn a way that allows you to enjoy tasks as you learn to manage them. It will increase your confidence, consistency, and habit stacking.

In this momentum cycle, the goal is for you to gain control over your past beliefs. This will allow you the space for momentum in your new and healthy habits and routines and eventually lead you to confidence in yourself, your abilities, and your power.

Toward the end of the lessons, you will feel most challenged because you must be equipped to maintain long-lasting habit changes. Without this, you'll revert back to your old ways, which is the biggest challenge for ADHD adults.

This is where CWB's habit stacking process continues to reinforce this. Habit stacking starts with small expectations and then builds the muscle memory of completing your routine. Once you're consistent, you can add more tasks!

Once you add new tasks to your routines, you will reach a whole new level of productivity and find a feeling of success. You will have the unique experience of testing your new routines in the real world while having the support, accountability, and challenge you need to achieve your next level of growth.

You'll learn how to prioritize your to-dos and to-don'ts, delegate unwanted tasks, and maintain forward consistency and momentum. This is about changing the way in which you show up in the world. You will show up with greater control, consistency, and confidence than you ever thought possible! No more being held back by your ADHD. You will be empowered by it!

"The 1% Rule: 1% progress + daily application (consistency) + persistence (focus) + time (endurance) = success."

—Tommy Baker

STEP 1: 1%

COACHING ENCOURAGEMENT

This is the part that most of my clients with ADHD want to skip. DON'T! It is imperative to start with the basics before even considering being productive.

I promise you will thank yourself at the end once you go through this step.

What has been chaotic in your mind lately?

What is something that you are not confident about doing?

At this point, you might be reading this book because you want to tame the chaos in your thoughts and physical space. They prevent you from focusing on what you want. They are taking up capacity in your brain.

Let's first start with some basics. Answer these questions:

- Am I getting enough sleep?
- Am I getting enough water?

- Am I getting enough nutrition?
- Am I getting enough exercise?
- Am I taking my medication consistently and is it working? (if this applies to you)

If you answered "no" to any of these questions, think of something *REALLY small* that you can do to take care of yourself! Maslow's hierarchy of needs is essential to understanding how to be at your optimal level. To make these ADHD-friendly, we have created the graphic below to help you achieve your basic human needs at a level that works with your brain. Consider if some of the options below will help you.

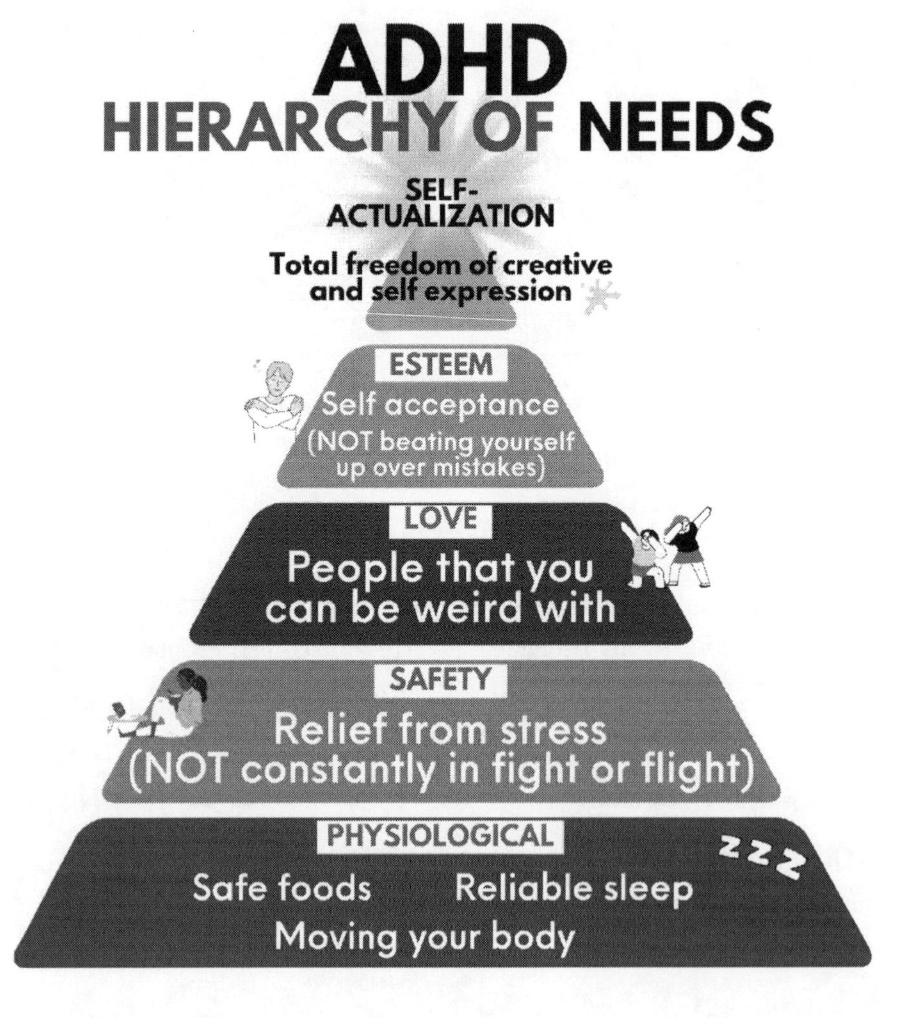

Start by choosing a small action in the category at the base of the pyramid. Instead of trying to reach your goal by taking action all at once, consider completing just that 1% of your goal each day. I call this the *1% Rule For You*. This picture visualizes the difference between taking really small steps instead of your current attempts to complete tasks.

On the left is the person taking small steps. Each rung on the ladder is a really small task that is achievable. On the right is the person who takes on huge chunks and jumps and jumps to grab that first rung. They keep jumping, but they never climb, and they never complete the task.

The importance of smaller steps

Do you jump out of bed and go straight to other people's agendas?

Most people do. We take a look at our phones, emails, social media, and text messages. When you do that, you start your day on other people's terms!

How did you and I start doing that? We don't know. This negative habit slowly developed in our lives without us realizing it. I call this "creep."

Anxiety can kick in when we are overwhelmed by our incomplete tasks. We can feel we woke up too late to get everything done. This also causes us to attend to other people's agendas as soon as we get out of bed.

DO NOT DO THIS!

When you wake up, do something that is for you.

What is something you can plan to do when you wake up that is for you? It can take as little as thirty seconds. Here are some ideas:

- Deep belly breathing.
- Drink a glass of water that you left by your bed.
- Listen to soothing music.
- Read something enjoyable.
- Stretch.
- Give yourself a high five in the mirror (as Mel Robbins suggests).
- Take a quick walk outside.
- Set your intentions for the day.

There are so many things you can do FOR YOURSELF. Don't pick one from that list because I told you to and allow me to set your agenda. Don't pick "giving yourself a high five in the mirror" just because Mel Robbins said to do it. Don't let her set your agenda.

You need to create nonnegotiables and boundaries. Picking one thing to do in the morning and sticking to it should become a nonnegotiable. Doing that sets boundaries. The phone and its notifications are not allowed during that time. If they were, they would be infringing on your boundaries.

Your Turn>>

What can you plan to do tomorrow morning and the next few mornings that is for yourself and is nonnegotiable and sets up boundaries? List three possibilities:

1. ______________________________

2. ______________________________

3. ______________________________

Of those three, which one will you do tomorrow morning?

____

Do that one for the next few days, and when you are consistently doing it, move on to step two.

COACHING ENCOURAGEMENT

I have provided blank lines for you after each step to help you take notes, write anything that comes to your mind while reading, or take a break by doodling before you implement the strategies given.

____

____

____

____

____

____

____

"The mind map will change your life."

—Tony Buzan

STEP 2: MIND MAPPING TO GET UNSTUCK AND CREATE ACTION

What is something that you have been stuck on recently, and you just cannot figure out a plan to break through it? (If you are stuck and need ideas, here are some common things that I have heard from clients that they have been stuck on and need help breaking through: how to make more money, when to exercise, what to focus on first during their day, how to actually spend quality time with their friends and family, how to pick and stick with a hobby, how to buy food that they will actually eat, how to go to bed in time to get reliable sleep.)

What thoughts come up for you when you think of being "stuck?" (You might be angry, frustrated, anxious, or uneasy.)

In this step I want you to list three to five things that hang over you because you need to get them done and haven't completed them.

1. ______________________________

2. ______________________________

3. ______________________________

4. ______________________________

5. ______________________________

Mind mapping visualizes your goals. Think of your goal like a chain. A chain has links. When you struggle to complete a specific goal, it is because you don't know how to link the links and create a chain.

We ADHDers tend to have lofty goals that have many steps and decisions that eventually overwhelm and frustrate us. They require too many executive functions. Consider taking that goal and simplifying it into smaller consecutive goals.

That is essentially mind mapping. The power of mind mapping is that it takes you from stuck to unstuck. It allows you to capture the chaotic cycle of thoughts and steps and goals that are storming in your brain and fasten them down on a piece of paper. Mind mapping shows that you have calmed that storm. That wasn't debris flying around in your mind. Those were brilliant steps and thoughts that you captured on paper. You harnessed their power and visually arranged them into a plan to reach your goal.

Mind mapping will help you explore other options, brainstorm, set goals, and create a plan. If this sounds overwhelming or unbelievable, here is a mind map I created as I was writing this book. Trying to be a new mom and author while remaining healthy and keeping up with my house became overwhelming. Here is what I wrote down.

MY MIND MAP EXAMPLE

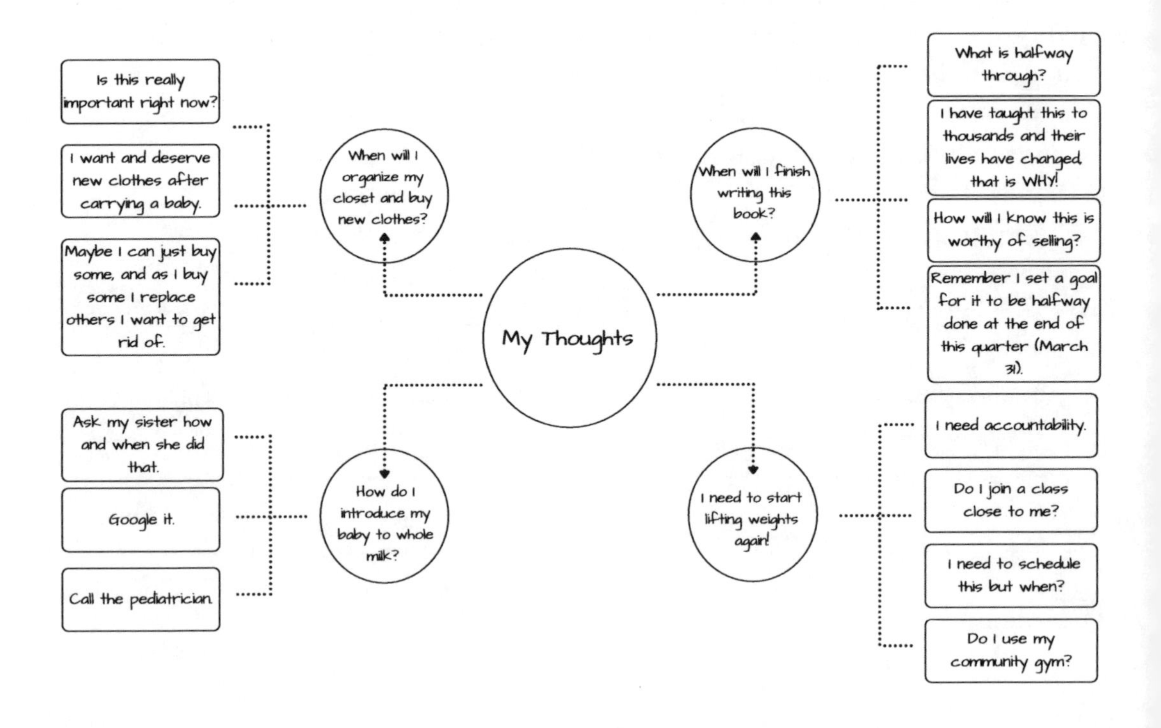

Your Turn>>

Now it's your turn to mind map your current thoughts! Look back to the three to five things that hang over you.

COACHING ENCOURAGEMENT

Remember: There is no right or wrong way of mind mapping. The idea is for you to get your thoughts out. Please don't overthink this. Just get your thoughts flowing. You might want to put on headphones to block out any extraneous noise and remove yourself from distractions while completing this exercise.

1. Use the outlined mind map on page 41 or a piece of blank paper.
2. Do not use lined paper.
3. Turn the book or sheet of paper to the horizontal landscape orientation.
4. In the middle of the page write "My Thoughts" in a shape of your choice. If you are using the outlined mind map on page 41, it is written in the circle for you.
5. Write your three to five thoughts around the middle. You don't have to place them as I placed mine. Put those thoughts in circles or clouds or boxes.
6. Brainstorm and let those thoughts flow. Write them down, drawing arrows from one box to another.

Here are some words of caution:

1. If you can't see multiple goals now, move on in the workbook. In a little bit, we will come back to your goals. Perhaps you can mind map then.

2. If starting a mind map is challenging for you, try this: first list your thoughts on the lines below or on a separate piece of paper and then transfer it to a mind map. You can group them by categories if you find that easier. I have created some space below for you to list your thoughts.

I HAVE INCLUDED A BLANK MIND MAP TEMPLATE THAT YOU CAN USE ON THE NEXT PAGE.

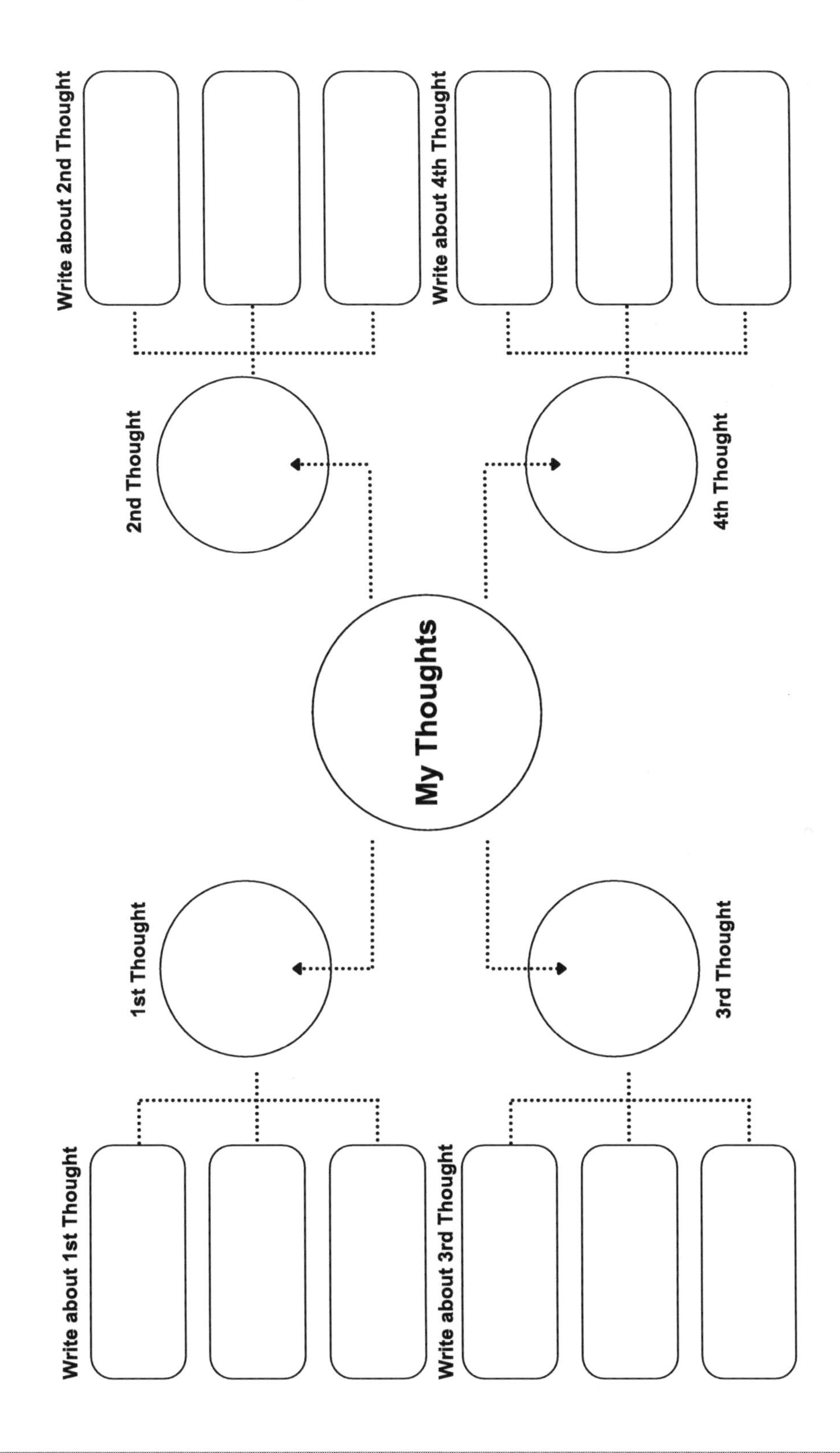
My Thoughts
1st Thought
2nd Thought
3rd Thought
4th Thought
Write about 1st Thought
Write about 2nd Thought
Write about 3rd Thought
Write about 4th Thought

Building Confidence

Do you want to be more confident in executing tasks?

That's what many of my clients say they want.

So, I ask them, "What comes to mind when you think of the word *confident*?"

What does a confident you look like?

Notice that I didn't put a blank line for you to fill in after that question. That's hard for us to answer because it's hard for us to visualize a confident self. Some of my clients will say, "I don't know how to be confident. That's why I am coming to you."

Dealing with this subject dredges up negative emotions, shame, and memories of failures. Even conceptualizing what you look like as a confident person can feel like another failure to add to your list of failures.

So some questions to spark the visioning process here might be:

1. What are some small things you can do **RIGHT NOW** that would make you start to feel confident? It can be LITERALLY ANYTHING. Write it down! Common examples are drinking water, going for a walk, brushing your teeth, making your bed, giving yourself a high five in the mirror, or standing in a superhero pose. List these out until you cannot think of any more examples.

____

____

____

____

2. Now that you have a **list of small items** you can do, I want you to pick **one small action item** that you are going to complete and work on. Right now you might be thinking, "How does this have anything to do with my actual vision of being confident?" Trust me, just continue to read and you will see how this comes to fruition.

   The one action item I am going to focus on this week is:

____

____

3. How am I going to be accountable for this action item?

____

____

Accountability Questions:

1. "*What* am I going to do?" (List the actual completed task below.)

____

____

2. "*When* will I have it done by?" (Write a date, day, and time.)

____

____

3. "*How* will I know I did it?" (What is your measure of knowing that you completed the task?)

____

____

I have added the fourth question to answer here to give us that extra boost of momentum:

4. "*How* will I hold myself accountable or enlist the help of others?"

Extra Space For Your Notes:

"Your time is limited, so don't waste it living someone else's life."

—Steve Jobs

STEP 3: LIFE CUPS

Do you nurture yourself as much as you nurture other areas of your life such as work, relationships, children, and your home?

If you answered "no" to any area of the previous question, what do you think is stopping you from taking care of yourself as much as everyone and everything else?

The Life Cup Assessment: Is your cup filled?

We are most deeply satisfied when our lives reflect what is most important to us. This book will help you identify what is important to you and teach you how to find satisfaction as you learn to focus on executing in these important areas.

We can use the life cup assessment in three important ways:

1. You can discover areas that need growth.

2. You create a visual aid for explaining where adjustments can be made to reach a balance.

3. The assessment can serve as a framework for annual planning.

You are going to rate your current level of satisfaction by coloring each cup to the level you currently are. The scale goes from zero (empty) to ten (full). If you are full, color the whole cup. If you are pretty empty and think you are a two, just color up to the two.

Some things to note:

- Don't overthink it! Put whatever number comes to your mind.
- It is hard to ever be a ten because we're always learning and growing.

COACHING ENCOURAGEMENT

If you don't understand what each cup means, do not worry.
I will explain them below.

Before you begin this exercise, it is important to consider what each life cup represents. Here are some factors that will help you determine the level to which you will fill your cup.

Home Environment: Are you feeling satisfied with the management of your household? Consider the following questions:

- Do you have an organization system in place?
- Are there certain roles within your household?
- Do you have meetings to make sure you are on the same page?
- Do you have food available for you?
- Are your bills paid?
- Is your house clean?
- Are things working properly?
- Is your house visually pleasing and organized?

Health/Fitness: This is not meant to lose or gain weight or put you on a diet! We all know the struggles that ADHDers can have with binge eating as we seek dopamine, forget to eat, have sensory issues surrounding food textures or taste, and/or are not hungry due to medication. If you are struggling with disordered eating,

I have added a secret chapter with recommendations for binge nutritionists that my clients have personally worked with to gain great results. This cup is meant to help you determine the following:

- Are you getting reliable sleep?
- Are you moving your body daily?
- Are you nourishing your body?

Significant Other/Romance: You might be in a relationship or not. Either is okay for this cup. Here are some things to think about in the significant other/romance cup:

- Are you embracing the imperfections of your relationship with yourself or your partner?
- Are you vulnerable?
- Are you making yourself and/or your partner a priority?
- Are you codependent or interdependent?
- Does your partner align with your core values and beliefs? (We will review this in chapter four.)
- How is your communication with your partner?
- Do you lift each other up?
- Do you know your partner's love languages and connect with them using their love languages?

Family: We can't choose our immediate family. Do you love your family? Consider the following questions:

- Are you satisfied with how you stayed in contact with family members?

- Do you spend quality time together?
- Do you set boundaries (if needed)?
- Do you know their love languages and connect with them using their love languages?

Friends: We are social beings. Regardless if you are an introvert or extrovert, isolating yourself can lead to serious health issues. Being around toxic individuals can also create a lot of stress. You are the average of the five individuals you spend the most time with. Here are some thoughts to consider when filling out your friend cup:

- Do you follow up with your friends and answer their messages or calls?
- Do you make plans to your liking?
- Are you happy with your friend circle?
- Would you like to make new friends?

Career/Purpose: Are you doing what you love? Are you energized by your day or constantly drained? Are you in the right work environment, do you have the right boss, are you over- or underwhelmed with the tasks you are given? Here are things to think about when filling out the career/purpose cup:

- Find a job that matches your strengths, values, and passions. (We will discuss these in the next two steps.)
- Ask others what they love about their job, what a normal workday is like, and what they don't love about their job.
- Get clear on what impact you want to have left the world when you die.
- Consider going after a promotion or learning new things!

Finances: ADHD tax, anyone? This is usually our least favorite area. Do you have control of your finances or are they controlling you? Are you in debt? Have you thought about retirement or investing? How about buying that house you have wanted for so long? Do you know what you are spending or earning each month? Are you budgeting? Here are things to think about when filling out the finance cup:

- Understand your expenses (use an app like Mint or QuickBooks to see what you have been spending the past few months).
- Get yourself out of debt by spending less and/or making more.
- Save up three to six months' worth of your expenses (as Dave Ramsey recommends).

Personal Growth: Are you inspired and feeling like you are being pushed outside of your comfort zone? Are you learning and expanding your mind? Here are some examples of personal growth:

- Completing and implementing the strategies in this book
- Getting coaches
- Reading
- Becoming a thought leader
- Doubling your income
- Traveling to a new place
- Adapting a growth mindset
- Being proactive
- Knowing yourself

Spiritual Growth: This helps you stay focused on mindfulness and/or religion. This goal can help you with stress and anxiety. Do you:

- Pray/meditate daily?
- Connect with a higher power?
- Visualize?

Ministry/Service: What are you doing to help others? This can be religious-based or secular. Here are some examples of ministry/services:

- Building community
- Volunteering
- Training new leaders
- Donating
- Mentoring
- Attending services

You will work on these cups over the next lessons. As you repeat this exercise, you will notice that other areas of your life are unintentionally improving because you focused on yourself.

Your Turn>>

Rate your current level of satisfaction by coloring each cup to the level you currently are. The scale goes from zero (empty) to ten (full). If you are full, color the whole cup. If you are pretty empty and think you are a two, just color up to the two.

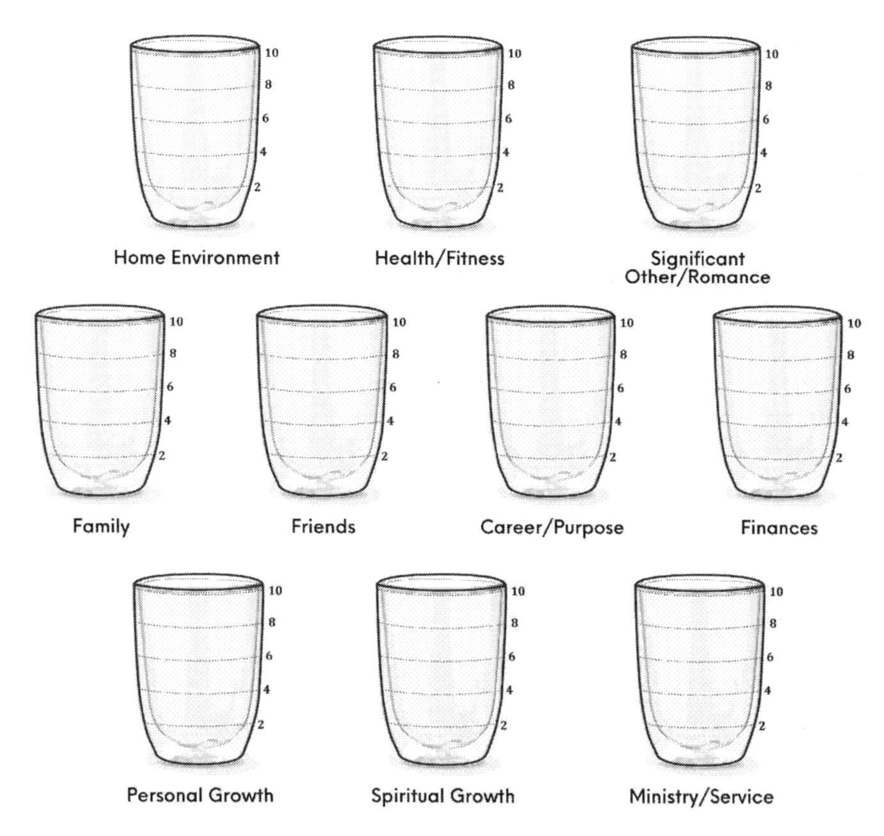

After you have filled your cups, pick the **top one to three areas** you would like to focus on over the next three months. This book will walk you through planning steps for your growth. Don't feel you have to pick three. You may only pick one.

For each cup you would like to work on, write the name on the top line and answer the questions below it.

Life Cup Category 1: ____

What number am I now? ____

What number can I be in a month? ______________________________________

Why am I stuck here?

____

____

How can I move forward?

____

____

What would a ten look like for me?

____

____

What action steps will I commit to?

____

____

Who can help me stay accountable? (i.e., friend, social media, coach, partner)

____

____

What structures can I put in place to ensure I move forward?

____

____

Life Cup Category 2: ____________________________

What number am I now? ____________________________

What number can I be in a month? ________________________

Why am I stuck here? ____________________________

____

How can I move forward?

____

____

What would a ten look like for me?

____

____

What action steps will I commit to?

____

____

Who can help me stay accountable? (i.e., friend, social media, coach, partner)

____

____

What structures can I put in place to ensure I move forward?

____

____

Life Cup Category 3: ____________________

What number am I now? ____________________

What number can I be in a month? ____________________

Why am I stuck here?

____

____

How can I move forward?

What would a ten look like for me?

What action steps will I commit to?

Who can help me stay accountable? (i.e., friend, social media, coach, partner)

What structures can I put in place to ensure I move forward?

Your Turn>>

<u>Directions</u>: Answer the questions below.

What was my biggest takeaway from this lesson?

Accountability Questions:

1. *What* small action will I take toward my goals? **You can pick a small action step or one thing from your mind map and work on it this week!**

____

____

2. *When* will I have it done by? (Write a date, day, and time.)

____

____

3. *How* will I know I did it? (What is your measure of knowing that you completed the task?)

____

____

4. *How* will I hold myself accountable or enlist the help of others?

____

____

Extra Space For Your Notes:

____

____

____

____

____

____

"Values are like fingerprints.
Nobody's are the same, but you
leave 'em all over everything you do."

—Elvis Presley

STEP 4: VALUES

Do you ever notice something taking place and feel uneasy about what has transpired? Leaving you to think, "That's not right!"

Where does that intuition/feeling come from?

Did you know that ADHDers generally have amazing intuition? Unfortunately, we don't trust our gut due to feelings of inadequacy, lack of confidence, people-pleasing tendencies, working memories, strong feelings of empathy, and circumstances from our pasts.

You need to harness the power of your gut. This will allow you to make decisions.

THESE GUT FEELINGS REPRESENT YOUR VALUES!

There are *hundreds* of values. Your values will differ from the values of your neighbors, friends, and family members.

Why do personal values matter?

They are unique to *you* and allow you to shine as your special self.

How do personal values lead to personal growth?

- When you understand your values, they become the key indicators of how you measure personal growth and development.

- When you believe you have achieved something, it is because you have implemented your personal value.
- You will be fulfilled when you assert your personal values instead of implementing someone else's personal values.
- Without identifying your personal values, you can continue to set goals and accomplish them but not personally develop them.

What can happen when you align your personal goals with your values?

1. Increased Motivation: When you set goals based on your personal values, your motivation skyrockets because you are focused on what is truly important to you.
2. Fulfillment: Achieving goals that reflect your personal values increases satisfaction and maximizes personal development.
3. Greater Accomplishments: Build your goals and dreams around your personal values and you will realize how much you can accomplish. The result is that you dream bigger and achieve more!

Directions: You are going to do an exercise to help you determine your personal values. This will require you to think back over your life and about those who have positively affected you. The takeaway from completing this exercise will be to identify personal values and discern if you are chasing these personal values in your goals.

Before you start this, I am sharing my example so you can see the process take shape. Remember, my values are probably not your values.

BROOKE'S EXAMPLE

STEP 1: List three people who have positively affected your life. You must know them personally (no celebrities, unless you know them), and they must be eighteen or over.

Name Mindy Relationship Mom

Name Bruce Relationship Dad

Name Gabe Relationship Husband

STEP 2: List three to five qualities that you admire about these people.

Name Mindy

1. Hardworking
2. Generous
3. Active
4. Loyal
5. Hustle

Name Bruce

1. Hardworking
2. Generous
3. Modest
4. Learning
5. Creativity

Name Gabe

1. Hardworking
2. Loyal
3. Creativity
4. Lifelong Learning
5. Active

STEP 3: Reviewing these qualities, cross out words that you feel DO NOT describe you. The ones you cross out are considered part of your values, but they are not core values because you do not possess them. They are not innate to you, but you may aspire to have them.

In the people I chose, I shared all of the same values. So in my case, I did not need to cross out any of their traits.

When you complete this activity you might need to cross out some of the values that you do not currently possess (even if you aspire to have them).

STEP 4: Group qualities that are similar. Narrow down and combine like values. Be sure that the concept of each combination is not lost or unclear. For example, "Authenticity/Honesty" are similar, but "Authenticity/Work Ethic" are not.

Group 1 of Similarities	Group 2 of Similarities	Group 3 of Similarities
• Hardworking	• Creativity	• Modest
• Active	• Lifelong Learning	• Loyal
• Hustle	• Learning	• Generous
⬇	⬇	⬇
Determined	Lifelong Learning	Caring

STEP 5: Write out the remaining values in the space below. These are your core values.

BROOKE'S CORE VALUES

1. Determined
2. Lifelong Learning
3. Caring

Your Turn>>

STEP 1: List three people who have positively affected your life. You must know them personally (no celebrities, unless you know them), and they must be eighteen or over.

COACHING ENCOURAGEMENT

Your values drive your decision-making, thoughts, actions, and goals. Do not skip this section unless you know your values and core values already.

If you cannot find three people who you admire, find three people you despise. Write the traits you do not like about them. To figure out your values and core values, you would write the opposite of the traits that you despise in them. Then you would categorize them into similarities and find your core values as we did in this activity.

Name ____________________ Relationship____________________

Name ____________________ Relationship____________________

Name ____________________ Relationship____________________

STEP 2: List three to five qualities that you admire about these people.

Name ____________________

1. ____________________
2. ____________________
3. ____________________
4. ____________________
5. ____________________

Name ____________________

1. ____________________
2. ____________________
3. ____________________
4. ____________________
5. ____________________

Name ____________________

1. ____________________
2. ____________________
3. ____________________
4. ____________________
5. ____________________

**The list below includes examples of values you may want to use to help.

Humor	Collaboration	Harmony	Nurturing
Partnership services	Friendship	Honesty	Beauty
Excellence	Creativity	Authenticity	Intelligence
Focus	Caring Nature	Empowerment	Romance
Recognition	Spirituality	Growth	Free Spirit
Accomplishment	Risk Taking	Performance	Peace
Action Driven	Elegance	Work Ethic	Drive
Success	Trust	Community	Joy
Wanderlust	Directness	Patience	Authority

STEP 3: Reviewing these qualities, cross out words that you feel DO NOT describe you. The ones you cross out are considered part of your values, but they are not core values because you do not possess them. They are not innate to you, but you may aspire to have them.

STEP 4: Group qualities that are similar. Narrow down and combine like values. Be sure that the concept of each combination is not lost or unclear. For example, "Authenticity/Honesty" are similar, but "Authenticity/Work Ethic" are not.

STEP 5: Write out the remaining values in the space below. These are your core values.

1. ______________________________ 2. ______________________________

3. ______________________________ 4. ______________________________

Your Turn>>

Directions: Answer the questions below.

What was my biggest takeaway from the core value lesson?

____

____

Accountability Questions:

1. *What* small action will I take toward my goals? Remember you can pick one small action or one thing from your mind map and work on it this week!

____

____

2. *When* will I have it done by? (Write a date, day, and time.)

3. *How* will I know I did it? (What is your measure of knowing that you completed the task?)

4. *How* will I hold myself accountable or enlist the help of others?

Extra Space For Your Notes:

"Offer your strengths to others and
you'll be amazed how many people
offer their strengths to you."

—Simon Sinek

STEP 5: STRENGTHS

Do you ever feel like you are constantly drained by what you are doing throughout the day?

Do you often feel stressed and anxious?

Have you ever heard of strengths?

I'm not talking about physical strength, I'm talking about your personal and character strengths. Peter Drucker said, "It's much easier to develop existing strengths than to work on weaknesses, and the payoff is dramatically better." Focusing on your weaknesses more than your strengths can lead you to anxiety, stress, and ultimately depression.

Your strengths are your gift to the world! Always lead with your strengths and align your activities with your personal values.

Character strengths are the positive parts of your personality that impact how you think, feel, and behave. Scientists have identified **twenty-four character strengths** that you have the ability to express.

Strengths come easily to you. Are you in a role that allows you to leverage and lead with those strengths?

If you continue to fix your weaknesses, you will encounter difficulty and dissatisfaction. Sure, you will improve over time, but is it enjoyable for you to spend the majority of your time working on something that may never become a strength?

Once you identify your strengths, you need to consider how you can use them in your everyday life. For instance, if your strength is connection, how can you use this outside of your job and integrate it into your hobbies and relationships?

Here are six benefits of knowing your strengths:

- Greater subjective and physical well-being
- Decreased depression symptoms
- Job satisfaction
- Engagement
- Less stress
- Increased positive affect

If you're using at least four of your top strengths in your job, hobbies, and daily life, you will live a more authentic life filled with intrinsic motivation, flow, positive experiences, meaning, and coping.

COACHING ENCOURAGEMENT

Throughout the rest of this workbook, I suggest you record weekly what activities have energized you, excited you, felt easy, felt peaceful, or brought positive energy. By answering and reflecting on these questions you can also determine what other strengths you might have. Unlike core values, strengths can change over time.

Your Turn>>

PART 1:
Please take ten to fifteen minutes to complete the VIA Character Strengths inventory at this website: viacharacter.org/character-strengths-via

This VIA survey will help you discover your strengths (although this is not the only way to identify your strengths). After completing the online survey, follow the steps below to complete the chart on page 73.

PART 2:
STEP 1: Under the "VIA" column of the chart on the next page, put an x for your Top 5 results received in the VIA Strengths Inventory.

STEP 2: Put an x for your Top 5 strengths that you believe you possess under the "Me" column.

STEP 3: Pick three people that you admire and trust (it could be the same three individuals you picked in lesson two).

Put their names under "Person 1," "Person 2," and "Person 3" on the chart below. Survey these individuals for their opinion of your top five strengths.

COACHING ENCOURAGEMENT

I highly recommend you reach out to each of the three people you choose individually and set up a time to speak with them in person or over the phone. There is a lot you will learn about how they perceive your strengths that will get lost if you do this only through text or email.

STEP 4: Add your x's from each row and write the total under the "Total" column.

Here is an example from a client who is now an ADHD coach. You can see why she went from failed restaurant owner to ADHD coach based on her strengths.

EXAMPLE CHART

			Person 1	Person 2	Person 3	
	VIA	Me	Mom	Coach	James	Totals
Appreciation of Beauty						
Bravery			x			1
Creativity	x	x	x		x	4
Curiosity		x		x		2
Fairness	x		x		x	3
Forgiveness						
Gratitude				x		1
Honesty	x	x			x	3
Hope			x			1
Humility	x		x			2
Humor		x		x	x	3
Judgement						
Kindness					x	1
Leadership						
Love						
Love of Learning						
Perserverance				x		1
Perspective	x	x				2
Prudence						
Self-Regulation						
Social Intelligence						
Spirituality						
Teamwork				x		1
Zest						

YOUR CHART

	VIA	Me	Person 1	Person 2	Person 3	Totals
Appreciation of Beauty						
Bravery						
Creativity						
Curiosity						
Fairness						
Forgiveness						
Gratitude						
Honesty						
Hope						
Humility						
Humor						
Judgement						
Kindness						
Leadership						
Love						
Love of Learning						
Perserverance						
Perspective						
Prudence						
Self-Regulation						
Social Intelligence						
Spirituality						
Teamwork						
Zest						

PART 3:

1. My top five strengths are … (These are your highest totals.)

1.______________________________ 2.______________________________

3.______________________________ 4.______________________________

5.____

2. Do my strengths correlate to my goals, jobs, hobbies, and responsibilities?

____

____

3. If I answered "no," what impact does that have on my life?

____

____

4. What changes can I make in my life to implement my strengths?

____

____

Your Turn>>

Directions: Answer the questions below.

What was my biggest takeaway from this lesson?

____

____

____

Which three people will I interview about my strengths?

Person # 1: ______________________________

Person # 2: ______________________________

Person # 3: ______________________________

Accountability Questions:

1. *What* small action will I take toward my goals?

____

____

2. *When* will I have it done by? (Write a date, day, and time.)

____

____

3. *How* will I know I did it? (What is your measure of knowing that you completed the task?)

____

____

4. *How* will I hold myself accountable or enlist the help of others?

____

____

Extra Space For Your Notes:

____

____

____

____

"Working hard for something we do not care about is called stress; working hard for something we love is called passion."

—Simon Sinek

STEP 6: FIGURE OUT WHY!

What are some ways you generally make decisions?

What usually gets you to take action on something?

Very often we do not understand the "why" behind why we started something. Look back several days, weeks, months, or years into a current project. You might not comprehend why you started.

These are all questions that you might ask yourself when you do not understand the "why" behind the genesis of a project:

- What got you so excited that you hyperfocused on this idea all this time?
- What motivated you to bring this project to life?
- What inspired you to work tirelessly toward this goal from the beginning?

Here's the answer to most of those questions. You started because the project appeared different and exciting. It's the shiny object syndrome.

However, that's a general answer. Before you begin your next endeavor, you want to answer "What was different?" and "What excited me?"

ADHDers can suffer from analysis paralysis. They can agonize over decisions and postpone or avoid making them. They might not have an approach for deciding or have criteria for making a decision.

Your Turn>>

Write Your Top One to Three Goals

(These would be what you chose in step three.)

<u>Examples:</u>

- What should I make for dinner?
- What is the next step in my business?
- How much money should I save?
- Should I buy, lease, or finance?
- Should I exercise today?
- What time should I wake up?

Goal 1: ____

____

Goal 2: ____

____

Goal 3: ____

____

Now answer the following questions for each goal below.

Goal 1:

1. What's the fear behind this goal or decision?

___

___

2. What information do I know to be true about my fear?

___

___

3. What information do I think I might need to make this decision/goal?

Goal 2:

1. What's the fear behind this goal or decision?

___

___

2. What information do I know to be true about my fear?

___

___

3. What information do I think I might need to make this decision/goal?

___

___

Goal 3:

1. What's the fear behind this goal or decision?

____

____

2. What information do I know to be true about my fear?

____

____

3. What information do I think I might need to make this decision/goal?

____

____

The key here is to **get to the core of why** you want to start something *before* you actually start it. Is it truly *you* who wants to do this? Are you instead wanting to do it because you are comparing yourself to others?

Have people you love told you that you *should* be doing this thing? Did you decide to do it because you trust them?

To get to the CORE of the WHY you're doing something, I have created this acronym to help you think about your reason:

> **C = Core:** Your goals should have meaning behind them. They should relate to your core values, your purpose, your strengths, or a challenge you're facing.
>
> **O = Oath:** Promise yourself that your goal is something *you* truly want and is not something your parents, friends, or significant other want.
>
> **R = Relevant:** Know *why* these goals are important to you.
>
> **E = Exciting:** You should see the value in your goals, be excited by them, and gravitate toward them.

I have copied a blank Why Funnel and an example of my Why Funnel below to help guide you when it's your turn to complete yours.

This is what the Why Funnel looks like:

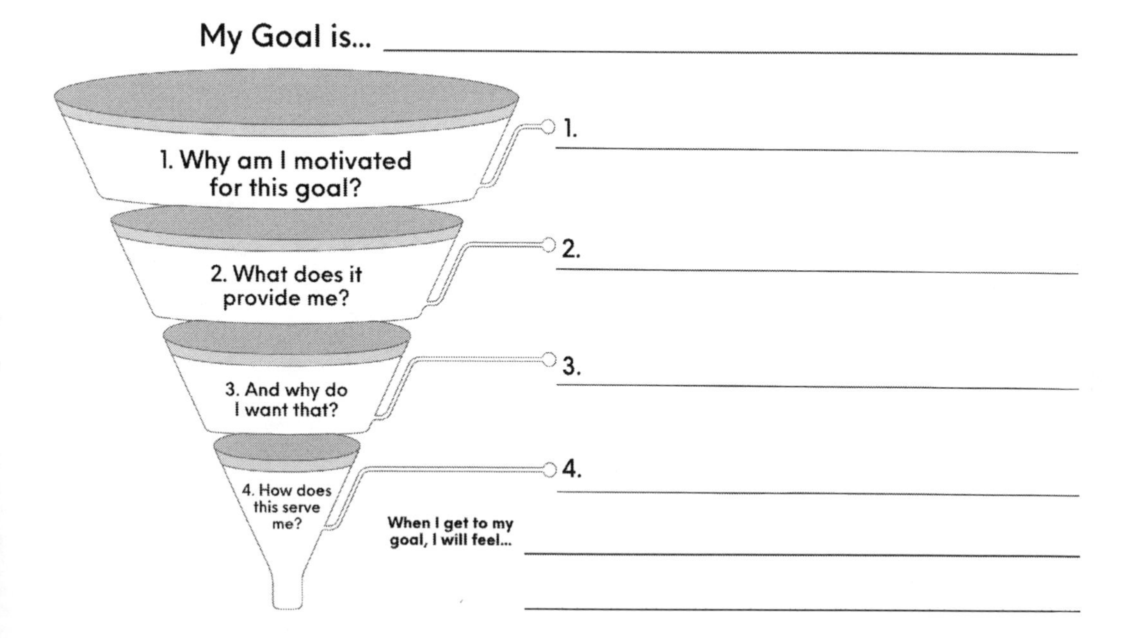

Here is an example of how to fill out the Why Funnel:

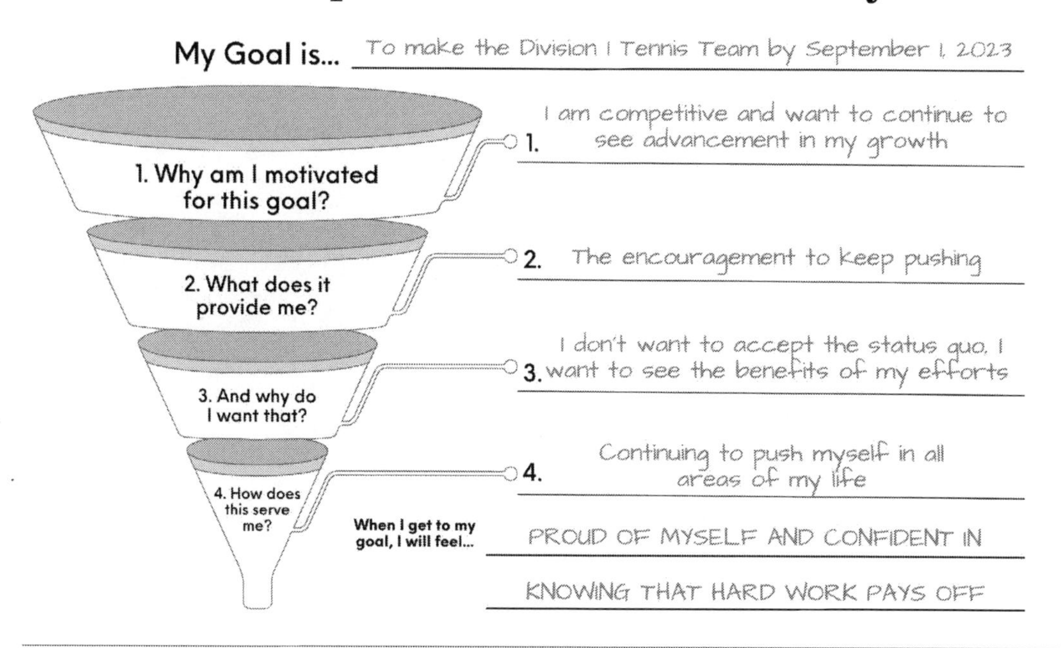

COACHING ENCOURAGEMENT

When you complete your Why Funnels, it is okay if you cannot answer each question. Don't overthink your answers. Each answer should stem from the question directly above it. Write down the first thing that comes to your mind.

Your Turn>>

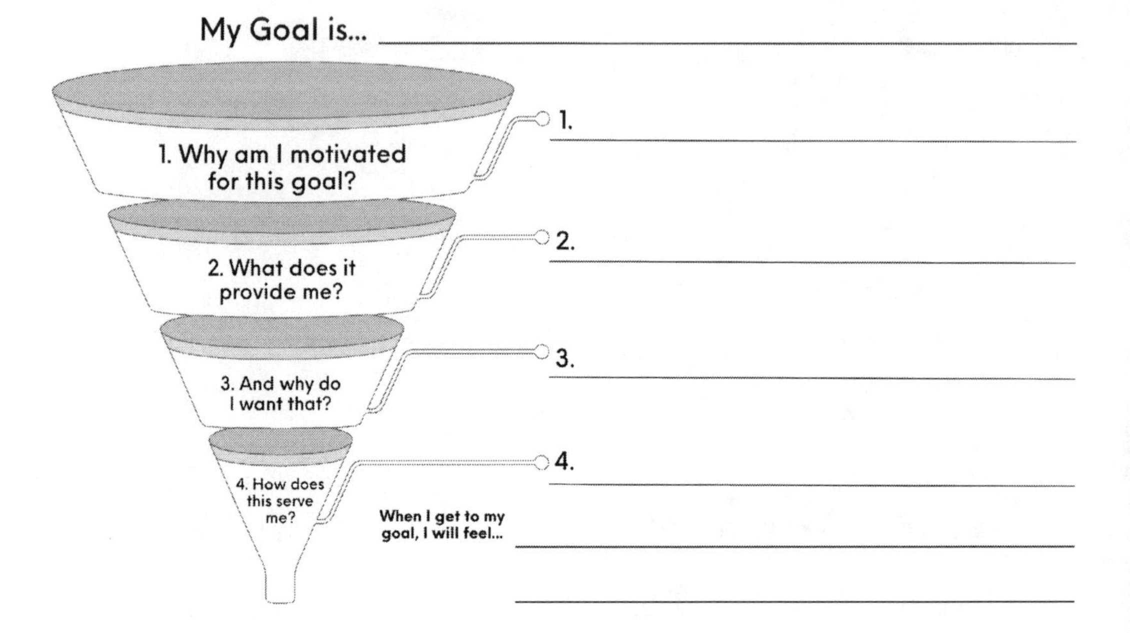

Your Turn>>

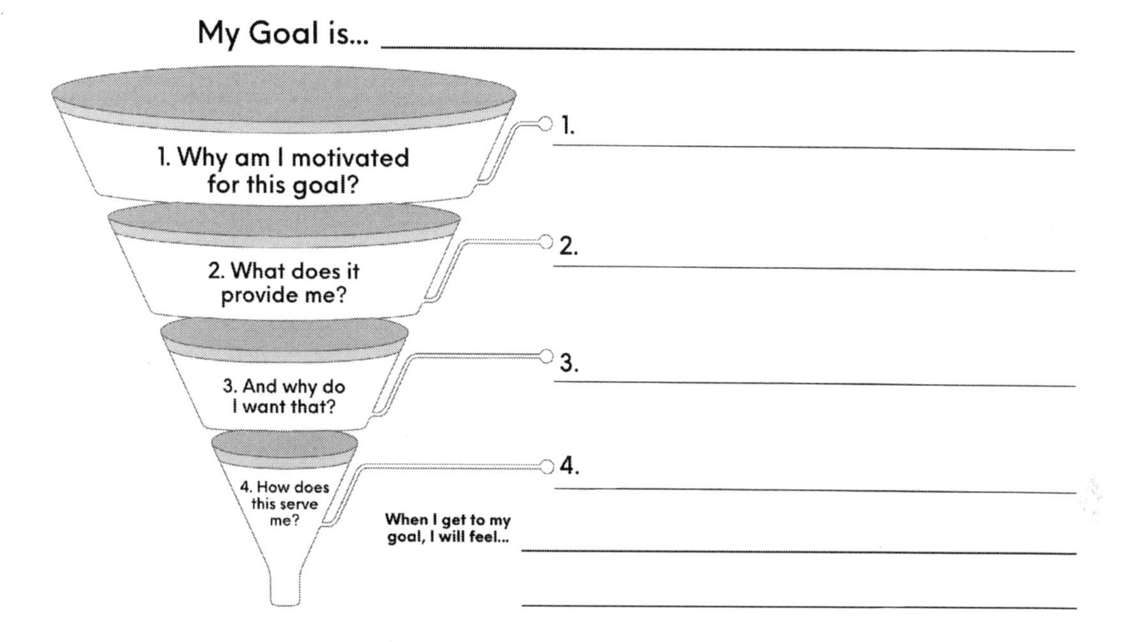
My Goal is...
1. Why am I motivated for this goal?
1.
2. What does it provide me?
2.
3. And why do I want that?
3.
4. How does this serve me?
4.
When I get to my goal, I will feel...

Your Turn>>

My Goal is... ______________________

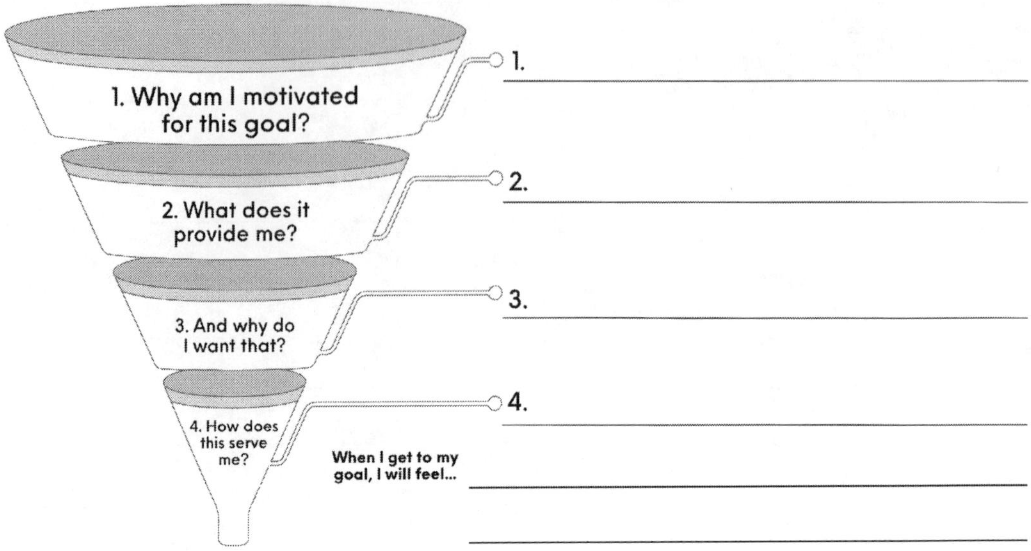

1. Why am I motivated for this goal?
2. What does it provide me?
3. And why do I want that?
4. How does this serve me?

1. ______________________
2. ______________________
3. ______________________
4. ______________________

When I get to my goal, I will feel... ______________________

____

<u>Directions:</u> Answer the questions below.

What was my biggest takeaway from this lesson?

____

____

In the past week or during this lesson, what activities have been energizing, exciting, easier, or peaceful? **(Each week, by answering this question you will learn more about your other strengths—some that might be different from your character strengths that you did in the previous step.)**

____

____

Accountability Questions:

1. *What* small action will I take toward my goals? **Remember you can pick a small action or one thing from your mind map and work on this week!**

____

---

2. *When* will I have it done by? (Write a date, day, and time.)

---

3. *How* will I know I did it? (What is your measure of knowing that you completed the task?)

---

4. *How* will I hold myself accountable or enlist the help of others?

"Setting goals is the first step in

turning the invisible into the visible."

—Tony Robbins

STEP 7: MAKE THEM SMART

Have you ever created a goal only to realize by the time you finished it was not realistic?

Do you believe you failed to reach the goal because of a problem with you and your performance?

In the previous step, we discussed our WHYs (which are from the CORE). We now need to discuss how to make them SMART.

S = Specific. Have a definite, clear goal. Instead of "I want to save more money," say something specific like, "I want to save $3,000 by the end of this year."

M = Measurable. Create a game plan. Whether it's laying out a schedule or crunching numbers, you'll find it easier to reach goals when you can see what you have done and what you need to do.

A = Achievable. Have a realistic goal. Arm yourself with tools to help make your goals achievable. Examples are a monthly budget, a planner, or supportive peers.

R = Relevant. Never forget why you're putting in the effort. It may become easy to get sidetracked and fall off course if you allow yourself to forget the reason for your hard work.

T = Time-Sensitive. Give yourself a time limit. Without a bit of time discipline, it can become easy to allow your goal to lose priority.

Here's an example of a SMART goal:

SPECIFIC—I want to wake up at six a.m. on weekdays.

MEASURABLE—I will record on a chart what time I go to bed and wake up.

ACHIEVABLE—I will text my best friend daily in the morning by eight a.m. after completion.

RELEVANT—I will have time for a morning routine before work and will feel centered and focused!

TIME-SENSITIVE—I will wake up at six a.m. Monday through Friday by December 15th.

Your Turn>>

Create one new goal or revise your existing SMART goals.

COACHING ENCOURAGEMENT

Remember: Your goal needs to be so specific and timely that you'll know how you did it, when exactly it will be done by, and what you will do to get there.

SMART GOAL INSTRUCTIONS

My SMART Goal:

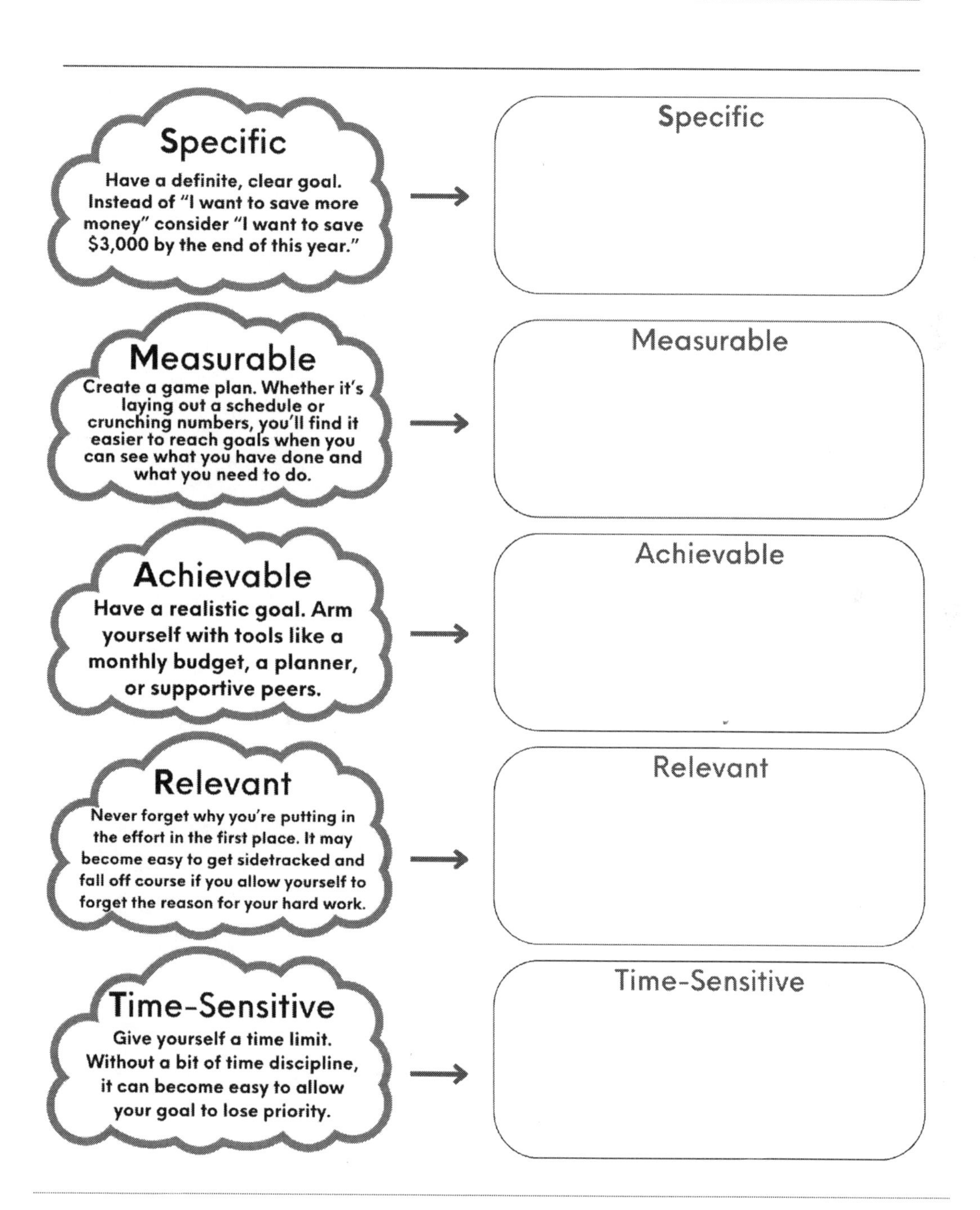

Directions: Answer the questions below.

What was my biggest takeaway from the SMART goals lesson?

____

____

In the past week or during this lesson, what activities have been energizing, exciting, easier, or peaceful?

____

____

Was my SMART goal different from my life cup goal?

____

____

If so, what do I think has changed?

____

____

How is knowing my values, strengths, and my "why" helping me get clearer on my goals?

____

____

Accountability Questions:

1. *What* small action will I take toward my goals?

___

___

2. *When* will I have it done by? (Write a date, day, and time.)

___

___

3. *How* will I know I did it? (What is your measure of knowing that you completed the task?)

___

___

4. *How* will I hold myself accountable or enlist the help of others?

___

___

Extra Space For Your Notes:

___

___

___

___

___

"When dopamine rises, so does your motivation to act."

—James Clear, *Atomic Habits*

STEP 8: DOPAMINE

Do you ever feel burned out? If so, when does this usually occur?

When do you usually feel the most focused?

Did you know that focus is directly related to dopamine? Dopamine is an essential neurotransmitter that allows us to regulate emotional responses and take action to achieve specific rewards. It is responsible for feelings of pleasure and reward.

If you have followed CWB's process up until this point, you are becoming a pro at taking action. This intrinsically makes you more motivated toward your actions, decisions, intentions, and goals. All of these increase your dopamine!

Individuals with ADHD have irregular levels of dopamine. You have a lot of it when you are motivated toward a goal. You have significantly less when you are not excited about the action or goal.

Dopamine is important to keep you focused on the task at hand. Let's check out some ways to increase your dopamine levels.

Ways to Increase Your Dopamine Levels:

ADHD medications raise the level of norepinephrine within the brain. Stimulants cause the brain to synthesize more norepinephrine. Nonstimulants slow the rate of norepinephrine being broken down. Once the level is where it should be, the brain functions normally, and you become less hyperactive, inattentive, and impulsive. Once the drug wears off, the level falls and symptoms return. According to Edward M. Hallowell, MD, "Medication helps about eighty percent of the time in the treatment of ADHD."

Neuroscientist Andrew Huberman says that what you do, how you do it, and how you conceptualize things lead to changes in dopamine. For instance, when you experience something very pleasurable, dopamine rises above the baseline and keeps you focused.

- Chocolate increases your dopamine by fifty percent, but the spike goes away after a few minutes.
- Sex (whether thinking about it or having it) doubles your dopamine.
- Nicotine (when smoked) briefly increases your dopamine 2.5 times.
- Amphetamines increase your dopamine by a factor of ten.
- Exercise can increase your dopamine. The result is subjective. If you enjoy exercise, you may double your dopamine. If you don't like exercise, you might have no increase or even drop below your dopamine baseline.
- Cold water exposure increases dopamine, and the levels are sustained for a while after you get out of the water.
- Caffeine slightly increases dopamine.

Dopamine levels are the primary component of motivation. When dopamine levels are low, neurons fire more than they should. Robert C. Spencer (as explained by Andrew Huberman, PhD,) states that "if dopamine levels are too low in the particular brain circuits, it leads to unnecessary firing of neurons in the brain that are unrelated to the task that one is trying to do and that is unrelated to the information that one is trying to focus on."

Your Turn>>

In order to optimize your dopamine, we have created a Dopamenu (a dopamine menu) below to give you options to help you increase your dopamine.

We have also included a blank one for you to fill in.

CWB DOPAMENU

Breakfast

Visualization
Stimulants
Coffee
Listen to music
Listen to a podcast
Eat protein
Probiotics
Lemon water
Exercise
Meditate/mindfulness
Cold water exposure
Jump around
Morning high five

Mid Morning Snack

Eat a snack
Jumping jacks
Listen to music
Listen to a podcast
Go outside
Consume almonds
Ginkgo
Power pose
Journal/write
Caffeinated tea

Lunch

Brisk walk
Deep belly breathing
Eat a snack
Listen to music
Listen to a podcast
Eat protein

Mid Afternoon Snack

Bath
Meditate/mindfulness
EFT
Listen to music
Listen to a podcast
Eat a snack
Go outside
Turmeric
15–20-minute power nap

Dinner

Get on a call with someone you like
Mindfulness
Eat protein

Dessert

Clean
Organize
Scroll social media
Watch a show you like
Plan a trip
Go on a vacation you're excited about
Practice safe sex
Brain dump
Get reliable sleep

MY DOPAMENU

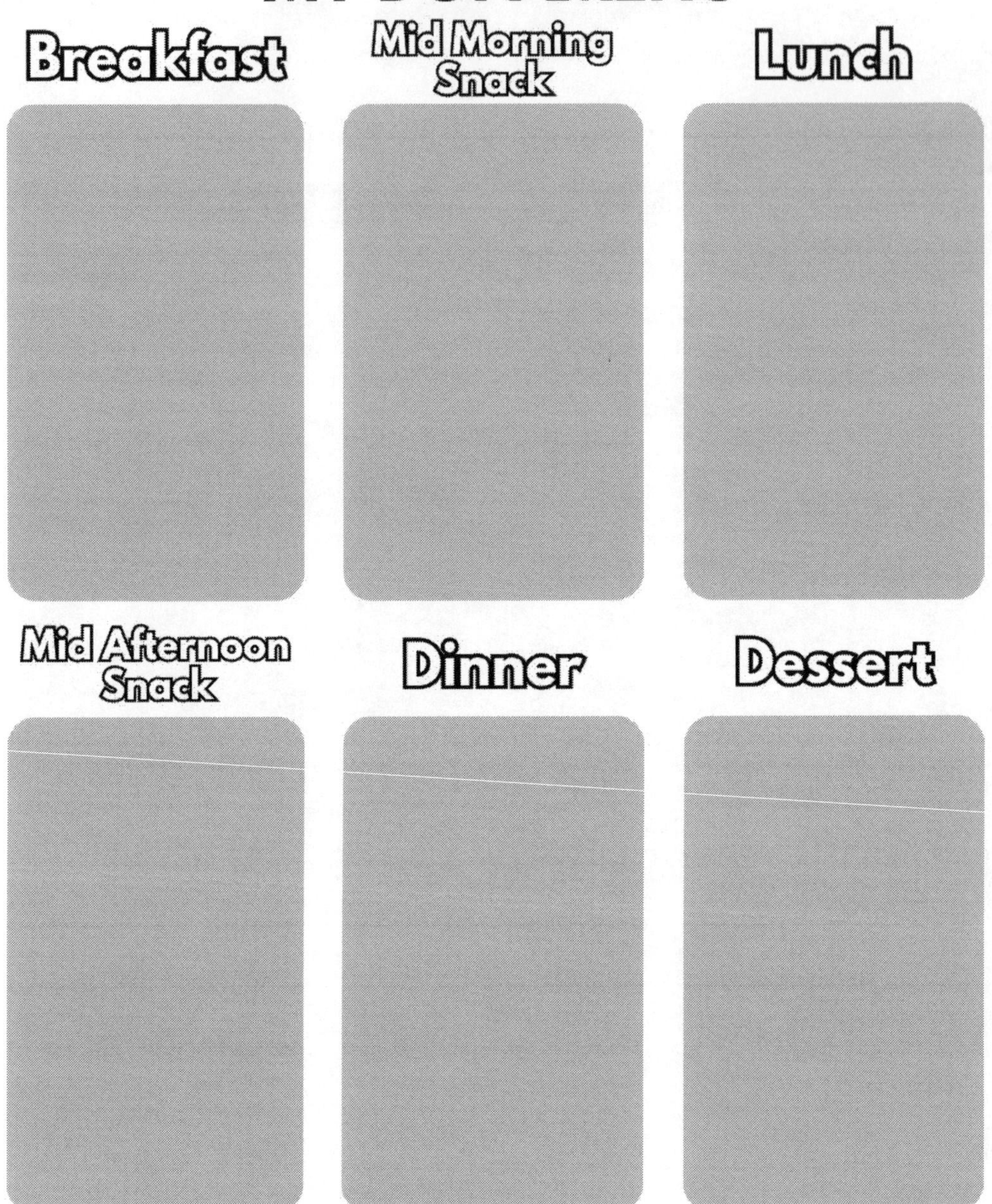
Breakfast
Mid Morning Snack
Lunch
Mid Afternoon Snack
Dinner
Dessert

We all have optimal focus times. It might be morning, afternoon, evening, or the middle of the night. You should utilize this time to do your most important tasks.

What is your optimal focus time? This is the time when you feel you have the most energy during the day. *This* is the time you should be completing your most important tasks!

Is it the *morning, afternoon,* or *evening*? Around what time is it?

COACHING ENCOURAGEMENT

In order to determine your optimal focus time, you can take notice and record when you feel the most focused and energized.

My optimal focus time is: ____

What dopamine-inducing activity above do I think works best for me? Write it below.

____

____

Your Turn>>

<u>Directions:</u> Answer the questions below.

What was my biggest takeaway from the lesson on dopamine?

____

____

In the past week or during this lesson, what activities have been energizing, exciting, easier, or peaceful?

____

____

Accountability Questions:

1. *What* small action will I take toward my goals?

____

____

2. *When* will I have it done by? (Write a date, day, and time.)

____

____

3. *How* will I know I did it? (What is my measure of knowing that I have completed the task?)

____

____

4. *How* will I hold myself accountable or enlist the help of others?

____

____

Extra Space For Your Notes:

"The lost time is never found again."

—Benjamin Franklin

STEP 9: ORGANIZATION

Do you ever feel like you lose track of time, so much so that you miss important appointments or forget to go to the bathroom, eat, or drink water?

Have you ever heard of time blindness?

Individuals with ADHD struggle with estimating time. We may overestimate (or very often, underestimate) how long something takes. Additionally, due to our executive dysfunctions, we can have a difficult time with planning, prioritizing, organizing, and scheduling.

We are usually *really* good at making lists. In fact, we often make *multiple lists* of the same items. Once we have made a list, we still have a hard time breaking down the action items and implementing the task.

- We might start something and not realize how many steps are involved.
- We might not have properly estimated time and become frustrated with ourselves because we are not progressing as fast as we expected.
- Our working memory may take a toll on our tasks. Since many tasks have multiple steps, we might have a hard time holding on to the step before and after our current step.

Due to our racing thoughts and constant motion, we might not peripherally see what actions we are taking. This can make it hard to see how to sharpen our focus and make real growth.

We tend to not detect what items are really dragging us down. We don't know how to avoid them and clear the chaos in our minds. Examples my clients have shared with me are unpaid bills, unpaid tickets (ADHD tax, anyone?), outdated designs, guilt, lack of self-care, exercise, frustrations, tasks left uncompleted, text messages owed, donations, and doctors' appointments.

Are you having difficulty focusing on what needs to get done throughout the day?

Do you live each day haphazardly, without a plan?

Do you feel weighed down by the number of tasks that build up on your to-do list?

I get it! I've been there, too. However, I have learned to stay focused on making and sticking to a plan. By using the proven tools and tricks in this workbook, I have improved productivity and continually produced greater results.

Many clients initially come to me and report that they need help managing their time. They tell me that they live each day without a plan. Their days are haphazard, stressful, and unproductive. In essence, I coach them through organization.

Your Turn>>

Let's start by thinking about what you currently do. How many of these ten items do you implement on a weekly basis?

1. To-Dos: (a) Determine your to-dos; (b) Keep track of your to-dos; (c) Schedule your day; (d) Look at your schedule.

2. Time yourself.

3. Take breaks.

4. Change your environment.

5. Exercise.

6. Set your morning routine.

7. Practice mindfulness.

8. Get reliable sleep.

9. Stay accountable.

10. Reward yourself.

Today we will learn how to implement some of the strategies above in our daily routine by learning about their impact and how to use them to be more productive. We will review CWB's world-renowned e-book, ***How to Focus by Focusing Your Time: 13 Ways to Be Productive***. I understand you might be confused that there are only ten listed above, but over time I ended up combining all of the steps from the to-dos into one section called "to-dos."

This e-book has been downloaded by tens of thousands of individuals with ADHD and has been taught to multimillion-dollar organizations including Chopra Global, ADDA, and CHADD, at the International ADHD Conference, and more.

Each of these steps is designed to provide you with practical strategies and insights that you can implement immediately. By incorporating these techniques into your daily routine, you will experience a significant boost in your productivity and overall sense of accomplishment.

Let's see how you can utilize the strategies to increase your organization through these ten steps.

Action 1a. Determine Your To-Dos

This action is crucial because it empowers you to gain clarity and effectively prioritize your tasks. By creating a comprehensive list of all your to-dos and breaking them down into smaller, more manageable tasks, you can ensure that nothing falls through the cracks. It's the foundation of productive and organized work.

Let me take you back to a time when I was constantly overwhelmed with my workload. Every day felt like a never-ending struggle to keep up with tasks, meet deadlines, and manage my responsibilities. The mounting pressure and lack of direction caused immense stress and anxiety, making it challenging for me to stay focused and productive.

I knew I needed a change, so I reached out for guidance and support, embarking on a journey to transform my approach to task management. Determining my to-dos became a pivotal turning point.

At first, the idea of writing down all my tasks felt daunting. I worried it would only amplify the overwhelming nature of my workload. However, I decided to trust the process and give it a try.

Sitting down with pen and paper, I began to pour out all my tasks onto the page. It was a cathartic experience, a way to visually confront the weight that had been dragging me down. Seeing my responsibilities laid out in front of me brought a mix of emotions—relief, apprehension, and determination.

But I didn't stop there. I realized that the sheer volume of my to-dos was part of the problem. I needed to break them down into smaller, more manageable tasks. So I rolled up my sleeves and started dissecting my to-dos into bite-sized pieces. Each task became a puzzle waiting to be solved.

What I discovered was truly remarkable. As I transformed my overwhelming list into a series of actionable steps, I felt a sense of control and empowerment growing within me. It was as if I was reclaiming my time and regaining the upper hand.

With my revised list in hand, I began separating three to five to-dos each day. I made sure to prioritize the most important task, the one that required my immediate attention and would contribute significantly to my progress. This simple act of prioritization became my compass, guiding me through each day with purpose and intention.

As I implemented these strategies, I noticed a profound shift in my mindset and productivity. I no longer felt paralyzed by the magnitude of my workload. Instead, I felt equipped with a clear plan of action and a roadmap to success. The whole process took me roughly forty-five minutes, but the time invested was well worth it.

My story is just one example of the transformative power of determining your to-dos. By taking the time to create a comprehensive list, breaking it down into smaller tasks, and prioritizing them effectively, you too can experience a newfound sense of clarity, control, and productivity.

Don't just take my word for it. Here's what Diane had to say about her experience: "Coaching With Brooke helped me gain clarity and create a system for managing my to-dos. Now, I feel more in control and productive."

Are you ready to embark on this journey of transformation?

Start by determining your to-dos and witness the positive impact they can have on your productivity and overall well-being.

Remember, every great achievement begins with a single step—the step of blocking off time to write out all of YOUR to-dos (every person's time is different).

Take that step today and activate your full potential.

Try doing this Sunday or Monday to set your week:

- List out all of your to-dos weekly.
- Break down your to-dos into more obtainable steps.
- Separate three to five to-dos daily.
- Circle, highlight, or underline one to-do that MUST be completed for the day.
- Keep this with you throughout the day to refer to and add to.

Action 1b. Keep Track of Your To-Dos

This step is crucial because it helps me stay organized and ensures that I don't forget important tasks. By keeping track of my to-dos, I can maintain a clear overview of my responsibilities and effectively manage my time. Let me share my own story of how I discovered the power of this step.

As a busy professional teaching in the New York school system, I'd regularly juggle multiple projects and deadlines. I would find myself overwhelmed and struggling to remember all the tasks I needed to complete. It was a constant source of stress and anxiety, causing me to feel scattered and unproductive.

I would receive phone calls from people asking me to honor commitments I had made. The rush of anxiety hit me like a tidal wave as I realized that I had dropped the ball AGAIN.

The pain of forgetting important tasks and missing deadlines took its toll on my work and personal life. I knew I needed to find a solution that would bring order and clarity to my daily tasks.

That's when I started implementing the practice of keeping track of my to-dos. I began using a digital task management tool that allowed me to create a comprehensive list of all my tasks, set due dates, and prioritize them effectively.

The impact was significant. By having a centralized system to capture and organize my tasks, I experienced a newfound sense of control and peace of mind. No longer did I have to rely on my memory or fear that something important would slip through the cracks.

With my to-dos neatly organized and prioritized, I could approach each day with clarity and focus. I no longer felt overwhelmed by the sheer volume of tasks. Instead, I had a clear roadmap that guided my actions and helped me make progress toward my goals.

The beauty of this step is that it can be tailored to your preferences and needs. Whether you choose to use a digital tool, a paper-based planner, or a simple checklist, the key is to find a system that works for you. It's about finding a method that allows you to keep track of your tasks effectively and ensures that nothing falls through the cracks.

By following this step, you can experience a remarkable transformation in your productivity and overall well-being. Life becomes easier as you have a clear overview of your responsibilities, a sense of control over your time, and the confidence that nothing important will be overlooked.

Are you ready to say goodbye to the chaos of forgotten tasks and missed deadlines?

Take the step to keep track of your to-dos, and activate the power of organization and productivity in your life. You'll be amazed at the difference it can make.

Once you determine your to-dos, where do you put them down and keep track of them?

Examples:

- Index card: Put all of your to-dos on one side and choose three to five of them to put on the other side. When you complete your three to five items, rewrite the to-do list on a new index card and put three to five items on the other side again.

- Jotter (same idea as an index card).

- Sticky notes.
- Planner Pad/Passion Planner/Bullet Journal.
- Notion.
- Asana/Trello/Monday.
- Google Tasks.
- Todoist.

Action 1c. Schedule Your Day

This step is essential for maximizing my productivity and ensuring that I make the most of my time. By scheduling my day, I can create a clear roadmap of tasks and activities, enabling me to stay focused and on track. Let me share my own story of how I discovered the power of this step.

During my time working in the New York school system, I was constantly bombarded with responsibilities, deadlines, and countless meetings. It felt like I was always playing catch-up, struggling to stay organized and meet everyone's demands.

Feeling overwhelmed and realizing that my current approach was not sustainable, I decided to implement a scheduling system. I turned to a digital calendar and task management app to help me manage my time more effectively. I started allocating specific time blocks for each activity, taking into account my priorities and the urgency of tasks.

As I began to schedule my day, I experienced a profound shift in my productivity and overall well-being. The simple act of setting aside dedicated time for each task allowed me to focus without distractions. It provided a sense of structure and clarity, ensuring that I tackled my most important responsibilities first.

By following my daily schedule, I felt more in control of my time and less overwhelmed by the chaos around me. I no longer had to constantly make decisions about what to work on next or worry about missing important deadlines. Everything was laid out before me, ready to be tackled one step at a time.

Implementing this step and finding a scheduling method that works for you, whether it's a digital calendar, a physical planner, or a combination of both, will help you take control of your day and make the most of your time. Scheduling allows you to allocate specific time for each task, manage your workload more efficiently, and create a sense of order and structure in your daily life.

Later, in the resource section, we will explore different apps that can assist you in scheduling and managing your time effectively. They offer various features and interfaces, so take the time to explore and find the one that aligns best with your preferences and needs. Remember, finding the right scheduling tool can greatly enhance your ability to manage your time effectively and stay organized.

Examples:

- Use this downloadable weekly schedule: (> *bit.ly/CWBschedule)*
- Electronic calendars:
    - Google Calendar
    - iCalendar
    - Tiny Calendar
    - Notion
- Use a planner (see which ones work for you):
    - Agenda book
    - Planner Pad
    - Passion Planner > *bit.ly/CWBPLANNER*

Action 1d. Look at Your Schedule

Taking the time to review my schedule is crucial for effective time management. By regularly checking my schedule, I ensure that I am aware of my upcoming commitments, deadlines, and priorities. Let me share my own experience to illustrate the power of this step.

During my journey to improve my productivity, I realized that simply creating a schedule wasn't enough. I needed to make it a habit to look at my schedule consistently and use it as a guiding tool throughout the day.

I started my mornings by reviewing my calendar and taking note of the essential appointments, meetings, and deadlines ahead. This helped me gain a clear understanding of what needed my immediate attention and allowed me to plan my day effectively.

As I continued to look at my schedule throughout the day, I became more proactive in managing my time. I could anticipate upcoming commitments, prepare for meetings in advance, and allocate sufficient time for important tasks. By regularly checking my schedule, I felt more in control and experienced a significant reduction in stress.

Gone were the days of feeling overwhelmed and constantly scrambling to catch up. By looking at my schedule regularly, I could plan my day strategically and stay on top of my commitments. It brought a sense of order and peace to my work life.

Incorporating this step into your routine and making it a habit to look at your schedule regularly will empower you to stay organized, make informed decisions, and effectively allocate your time and energy. It allows you to proactively manage your commitments and ensure that you are on track to achieve your goals.

Check your schedule a *MINIMUM* of three times each day:

- In the morning
- Throughout the day (at lunch)
- At night before you go to sleep

Action 2: Time Yourself

As described by Julia Gifford for The Muse, working for long periods of time can be detrimental to your level of engagement with a certain task.

Timing myself has been a game-changer in managing my time effectively and boosting productivity. By tracking the time spent on different tasks, I gain valuable insights into my work habits and can allocate my time more efficiently. Let me share my own experience of discovering the power of this step.

As a student, I often found myself struggling to complete assignments and study within the allotted time. I would frequently face the stress of impending deadlines and the frustration of feeling like I didn't have enough time. Determined to find a solution,

I decided to start timing myself while working on various tasks.

I began using a timer app on my phone that allowed me to set specific time intervals for each task. Whether it was writing an essay or studying for an exam, I would activate the timer and immerse myself fully in the task at hand. This simple act of timing myself brought about a remarkable shift in my productivity.

By tracking my time, I became acutely aware of how long different tasks actually took. I noticed patterns of inefficiency, such as spending excessive time on certain activities or getting distracted frequently. This newfound awareness empowered me to make conscious adjustments and find strategies to optimize my workflow.

Timing myself not only increased my productivity but also instilled a sense of urgency and focus in my work. Knowing that I had a set time limit pushed me to stay on track and avoid unnecessary distractions. It helped me develop discipline and prioritize tasks more effectively.

This comment came from Jessica, a client: "I used to feel overwhelmed by the amount of work I had to do, but timing myself has been a game-changer. It has made me more aware of my time usage and motivated me to stay focused. Now, I can complete tasks more efficiently and have better control over my schedule."

To effectively time yourself, there are various apps available that are specifically designed for time tracking and productivity enhancement. These apps offer features like setting timers, tracking activity duration, and providing insights into time usage. By exploring these tools, you can find the one that best suits your needs and preferences.

By incorporating the practice of timing yourself into your routine, you can develop a greater awareness of your time usage, improve focus, and accomplish tasks within desired time frames. It's a simple yet powerful technique that can significantly enhance your productivity and help you make the most of your valuable time.

Examples:

- Kitchen timer: This will help you to hear the ticking of time passing.
- Pomodoro apps: The Pomodoro Technique can be found on multiple apps, and you can set twenty-five-minute intervals with five-minute breaks that can be logged.
- Time Timer: Visual method of seeing time move.

- Set a timer on your phone or on your virtual home assistant (i.e., Alexa, Google Home).

- Put up analog clocks in areas where you complete work in order to watch the time more closely and hear the ticking.

Action 3: Take Breaks

According to Julia Gifford for The Muse, repeating tasks leads to cognitive boredom, which in turn halts your ability to thrive at the task at hand. The human brain isn't able to focus for eight hours at a time.

Taking breaks is essential for maintaining focus, recharging energy, and maximizing productivity. I learned the importance of incorporating regular breaks into my work routine during my time as a dedicated professional in the demanding New York school system. Working continuously without breaks led to diminishing energy levels and a decline in concentration as the day progressed.

Realizing the need for a change, I decided to experiment with taking short breaks throughout my workday. After every sixty minutes, I would set a timer and commit to a five-minute break. During these breaks, I would stretch, take a short walk, or simply relax and clear my mind.

To my surprise, I experienced a significant improvement in productivity and focus. By giving myself regular breaks, I felt more refreshed and revitalized. I discovered that I could maintain a higher level of concentration for longer periods and accomplish tasks more efficiently.

Matthew, a client, had the same realization. He said, "I used to believe that pushing through without breaks was the key to productivity. But taking short breaks has completely changed my perspective. I feel more energized, focused, and productive. It's amazing what a few minutes of rest can do for your overall performance."

Taking breaks is not about slacking off or wasting time. It's about giving your mind and body a chance to recharge and maintain optimal functioning. Here are three strategies that I found effective in incorporating breaks into my routine:

- Pomodoro Technique: The Pomodoro Technique involves working in focused bursts, typically twenty-five minutes, followed by a short break of five minutes. After completing a set of four pomodoros, I would take a more extended break, around fifteen to thirty minutes. This technique helped break tasks into manageable chunks and prevented burnout.

- Active Breaks: Instead of mindlessly scrolling through social media or watching videos during breaks, I engaged in activities that promoted physical movement and mental relaxation. I would stretch my body, do a quick exercise routine, practice deep breathing, or listen to calming music. These activities helped rejuvenate my mind and increase my overall well-being.

- Change of Environment: Sometimes, a change of scenery can be refreshing and invigorating. I would step away from my workspace and go outside for a breath of fresh air. I took short walks in nature, found peaceful spots in nearby parks, or simply sat in a different area of my home or office. The change in environment stimulated my senses and provided a mental reset.

Remember, incorporating effective breaks is an essential part of maintaining productivity and preventing burnout. By implementing strategies like the Pomodoro Technique, engaging in active breaks, and seeking a change of environment, you can optimize your break time and come back to your tasks with renewed focus and energy:

More on Breaks:

- Stretching can help the flow of oxygen increase.

- Go outside. Studies show that just spending time in nature can help alleviate mental fatigue by relaxing and restoring the mind. Additionally, increased exposure to sunlight and fresh air helps increase productivity and can even improve your sleep.

- Drink water or eat a snack.

- Take some deep breaths.

Action 4: Change Your Environment

According to neuroscientists, the connections your brain makes between the study material and your various working/study environments will help you retain the information and recall it better. You will break the monotony of studying/working in the same space, and you will improve your productivity.

As I navigated my career in the bustling New York school district, I discovered a transformative secret to enhancing my focus and productivity: changing my environment. Amid the demands of my work, I often found myself battling distractions and struggling to maintain a deep level of concentration. It became evident that the familiar sights and sounds of my office hindered my ability to stay fully engaged with my tasks.

Determined to find a solution, I decided to venture beyond the confines of my usual workspace. I sought refuge in the vibrant cafés scattered throughout the city, embracing the energy and buzz of these new surroundings. With my laptop and essential materials in tow, I settled into a cozy corner and began my work.

The change in environment breathed fresh life into my productivity. The hustle and bustle of the café created a gentle background hum that propelled me forward. Surrounded by the quiet chatter of fellow patrons and the aroma of freshly brewed coffee, I found myself more focused and more immersed in my work than ever before.

Within this dynamic setting, I discovered an invigorating sense of purpose and clarity. The novel environment helped me break free from the monotony of my office and infused my work with a newfound energy. It became my sanctuary, a place where distractions faded into the background and my creativity flourished.

Changing your environment doesn't necessarily mean venturing outside your home or office. Consider these strategies to optimize your surroundings:

- Create a Dedicated Workspace: Carve out a designated area in your home or office solely dedicated to your work. Transform it into a space that inspires and motivates you, free from distractions and clutter. By having a dedicated workspace, you create a mental shift that signals your brain to focus and be productive.

- Personalize Your Environment: Surround yourself with elements that ignite your creativity and drive. Decorate your workspace with meaningful objects, artwork, or plants that resonate with your vision and purpose. Customizing your environment can evoke a sense of ownership and comfort, further enhancing your productivity.

- Explore Alternative Settings: If your usual workspace becomes stagnant, venture out and explore new environments. Visit a local park, a cozy library, or a communal workspace. By changing your surroundings, you stimulate your senses and invite fresh perspectives into your work.

Embrace the power of your surroundings, wherever they may be, and activate your full potential. By intentionally changing your environment to minimize distractions and create a focused atmosphere, you can elevate your productivity, unleash your creativity, and embark on a journey of enhanced performance. Allow your environment to become a catalyst for your success.

More on Changing Your Environment:

- Change room/conditions: Sometimes different settings, lighting, and noises can help you focus.
- Leave your house: Go to a library, bookstore, or coffee shop. (BONUS: This can help you feel accountable by getting the effect of body doubling.)
- Take your work outside. (BONUS: vitamin D and serotonin boost)

Action 5: Exercise

Chris Bailey shares the benefits of exercise to boost your focus below:

- Exercise is one of the easiest ways to reduce fatigue, boost energy, and increase your productivity throughout the day. Researchers discovered that just ten minutes of exercise is enough to boost memory and attention performance throughout the day.
- Exercise produces "positive changes in concentration, stress, energy, and well-being."
- Exercise increases blood flow to your brain, improving your mental cognition and ability to focus.
- Exercise creates new brain cells.

- Exercise works out your attention muscle and improves the "brain circuits that underlie your ability to think."

- Exercise enhances your mood, impulse control, memory, and energy levels, which are all factors that influence how focused you are.

- Aerobic exercise improves your focus the most. It also has the greatest ability to improve decision-making ability.

- Do not only do aerobic exercise. Although cardio may be best for your focus, balancing a few exercise types, like yoga, weight training, and cardio, will make you the most focused. This lets you reap the benefits of all types of exercise.

- Don't over-train! According to Scott Scheper, the author of *How to Get Focused*, "As soon as you push yourself beyond a certain limit, your alertness will significantly drop." Not over-training will keep you running at your peak.

Activating my full potential and boosting my productivity was a journey that led me to discover the transformative power of exercise. As a busy professional navigating the demands of my work, I often found myself struggling to maintain focus and energy throughout the day. Determined to find a solution, I made a life-changing decision—to prioritize exercise as an integral part of my daily routine.

Embracing this commitment, I devoted thirty minutes each morning to engaging in physical activity. Whether it was a walk around Central Park, a challenging workout session, or some yoga, it didn't take much to feel the immense value of moving my body and igniting my energy.

Despite initial challenges in finding time and motivation (which happens to all of us), I persisted, knowing that the benefits of exercise would far outweigh any obstacles.

To my delight, I experienced a significant shift in my overall well-being, focus, and productivity. Regular exercise not only enhanced my physical fitness but also revitalized my mental state. I noticed increased alertness, improved problem-solving skills, and a sustained ability to concentrate on tasks for extended periods.

The decision to prioritize exercise in my daily routine was a game-changer. It transformed not only my physical fitness but also my mental clarity and productivity.

I now feel invigorated, focused, and equipped to conquer any challenge that comes my way. It's remarkable how a small investment of time in exercise can yield such profound returns. Discipline is reinforced by having an accountability partner to help ensure that I stay consistent.

Incorporating exercise into my daily routine didn't have to be complicated or time-consuming. I discovered three practical strategies that helped me make exercise a consistent part of my life:

- Discover Enjoyable Activities: I found physical activities that brought me joy and fulfillment. Whether it was basketball, swimming, jogging, or tennis, choosing activities I genuinely enjoyed made exercise more enticing and sustainable in the long run.

- Schedule Exercise Sessions: I treated exercise as an essential appointment with myself. I set aside dedicated time in my daily or weekly schedule specifically for physical activity. By prioritizing and scheduling exercise in advance, I increased the likelihood of following through and reaping the benefits.

- Start Small and Progress Gradually: If you're new to exercise or haven't been physically active for a while, it's important to start with manageable steps. I began with shorter exercise sessions and lower-intensity activities, gradually increasing the duration or intensity as I built strength and endurance. Taking it one step at a time ensured a sustainable and safe approach to exercise.

By incorporating regular exercise into my life, I invested in my physical and mental well-being, optimizing my cognitive abilities and activating my full potential. Discovering enjoyable activities, scheduling exercise sessions, and starting small were key elements of my journey. I embraced the transformative power of exercise and experienced the positive impact it had on my focus, energy, and overall productivity.

Action 6: Set Your Morning Routine

Establishing a morning routine sets the tone for the rest of your day and can significantly impact your productivity and overall well-being. By intentionally designing your mornings to be purposeful and nourishing, you can create a solid foundation for a productive and fulfilling day ahead.

Let me tell you the story of my client, Megan, who discovered the power of setting a morning routine.

Megan used to dread mornings. She would hit the snooze button multiple times, rush through getting ready, and often found herself feeling scattered and overwhelmed before the day had even begun. This chaotic start left her feeling stressed and unprepared to tackle her tasks effectively.

One day, Megan decided to take control of her mornings and implement a consistent morning routine. She recognized the importance of starting the day on a positive and intentional note. She began by waking up earlier and allowing herself ample time to engage in activities that nurtured her mind, body, and spirit.

Her morning routine included activities such as meditation, journaling, stretching, and enjoying a nutritious breakfast. Each activity was carefully chosen to promote mindfulness, clarity, and a sense of inner calm. Megan found that this intentional start to her day helped her feel grounded, focused, and ready to tackle her priorities with greater clarity and purpose.

Megan once told me, "I used to rush through my mornings, feeling frazzled and disorganized. Implementing a morning routine has completely transformed my day. I now have dedicated time for self-care and reflection, which sets a positive tone for the rest of the day. It has made a remarkable difference in my productivity and overall well-being."

Setting a morning routine doesn't have to be complicated or time-consuming. Here are three elements you can incorporate into your morning routine to help you start the day on a positive note:

- Mindfulness Practice: Begin your day with a few minutes of mindfulness practice such as meditation or deep breathing exercises. This allows you to cultivate a calm and focused mindset, enabling you to approach the day with greater clarity and presence.

- Journaling or Visualization: Take a few moments to jot down your thoughts, gratitude, or intentions for the day in a journal. Alternatively, you can engage in visualization exercises, visualizing your goals and desired outcomes. This helps you set a positive and focused mindset for the day ahead.

- Movement or Exercise: Incorporate some form of physical activity into your morning routine. It could be a quick stretching routine, a short walk, or a workout session. Physical movement not only boosts your energy level but also enhances your mental clarity and prepares you for the day ahead.

By setting a morning routine that aligns with your values and priorities, you can establish a positive and empowering start to your day. Experiment with different activities and find what resonates with you. Remember, it's not about the length of your routine but the intention behind it. Embrace the power of a morning routine and experience the positive impact it can have on your focus, productivity, and overall well-being.

Start your day with intention by implementing one or more of these strategies:

- Exercise.
- Take a quick walk outside.
- Mindfulness.
- Journal.
- Visualize.
- Stretch.
- Look at your planner.
- Drink a glass of lemon water when you wake up.
- Eat a nutritious breakfast that includes fat and protein.

Action 7: Practice Mindfulness

My friend and neuroscience researcher, Shannon Sanguinetti, MSc, says that a light workout/meditation will help redirect blood flow away from brain regions not required for attention and into the limbs. Follow this with getting right into the task you want to accomplish. This will help with completing the task because your body will selectively allocate oxygenated blood to the brain regions required for focus.

Embracing mindfulness is a powerful step toward enhancing focus, reducing stress, and fostering a greater sense of well-being. By cultivating a state of present-moment awareness, you can bring clarity, calmness, and intention to your daily life.

As someone who used to struggle with feeling overwhelmed and distracted, I discovered the transformative effects of embracing mindfulness. Recognizing the need to find balance and inner peace, I began exploring mindfulness practices.

I was tired of realizing that I wasn't present when with friends or family. My mind was elsewhere—always thinking about some other project or conversation that I had with someone else. It just became known among my friends and family that I was a daydreamer. However, the thoughts were usually soaked in anxiety, so it wasn't a good dream but a stress inducer. It added insult to injury that I wasn't even present with the ones that I loved and who wanted to be with me.

I started by incorporating short mindfulness exercises into my daily routine. Taking a few minutes each day to focus on my breath, observe my thoughts without judgment, and bring my attention fully to the present moment allowed me to deepen my mindfulness practice. Over time, I experienced a profound shift in my well-being and productivity. It started to become a new habit and I felt the reduction of stress. It became uplifting to feel this daily.

Through mindfulness, I gained the ability to pause, observe my thoughts and emotions, and respond intentionally rather than reactively. This newfound awareness allowed me to navigate challenges with greater ease and make more informed decisions. By staying present in each moment, I could fully engage in my tasks, connect more deeply with others, and experience a greater sense of fulfillment.

Embracing mindfulness doesn't have to be complicated. Here are three simple practices you can explore to cultivate mindfulness:

- Breath Awareness: Take a few moments throughout your day to bring your attention to your breath. Notice the sensations of inhaling and exhaling, allowing your breath to anchor you in the present moment.

- Body Scan: Set aside time to perform a body scan meditation. Start from the top of your head and gradually move down, bringing your awareness to each part of your body. Notice any sensations or areas of tension and gently release and relax as you breathe.

- Mindful Activities: Engage in everyday activities with mindfulness. Whether it's drinking a cup of tea, walking in nature, or washing dishes, bring your full attention to the experience. Notice the sights, sounds, textures, and sensations involved, immersing yourself fully in the present moment.

By embracing mindfulness, you can enhance your focus, reduce stress, and cultivate a greater sense of well-being. Incorporate simple mindfulness practices into your daily routine and observe the positive impact it has on your productivity, relationships, and overall quality of life.

More Mindfulness Examples:

- Stretching
- Taking deep breaths
- Push-ups
- Squats or any five-minute workout that you enjoy
- Yoga

Action 8: Get Reliable Sleep

Quality sleep plays a crucial role in our overall well-being and productivity. When we prioritize sleep and establish healthy sleep habits, we set ourselves up for success in various aspects of our lives.

I used to struggle with my sleep patterns. I still do from time to time (especially if my husband is snoring). I would stay up late, scrolling through my phone, worrying about unfinished tasks, or going down social media rabbit holes that seemed to never end.

Minutes would turn into an hour or two. I'd look at the clock and my anxiety would rise. I would put the phone down, but then my thoughts would start racing. I'd wake up feeling exhausted and groggy. My lack of quality sleep not only affected my energy levels but also impaired my focus, memory, and decision-making abilities.

Realizing the impact sleep had on my daily life, I decided to make a change. I asked myself:

- How can I create a bedtime routine that helps me wind down and prepare for sleep?
- What steps can I take to establish a consistent sleep schedule, even on weekends?
- How can I create a sleep-friendly environment in my bedroom to promote restful sleep?

Prioritizing reliable sleep has been transformative for me. I now wake up feeling refreshed and rejuvenated, ready to tackle the day ahead. My ability to focus and concentrate has improved, and I feel more mentally sharp and alert throughout the day.

To establish reliable sleep habits, I suggest considering the following practices:

- Consistent Sleep Schedule: Set a consistent sleep schedule by going to bed and waking up at the same time every day, including weekends. This helps regulate your body's internal clock and promotes better sleep quality.
- Bedtime Routine: Establish a relaxing bedtime routine to signal your body that it's time to unwind and prepare for sleep. Consider activities such as reading a book, taking a warm bath, practicing relaxation techniques, or listening to calming music.
- Sleep-Friendly Environment: Make your bedroom a sanctuary for sleep. Ensure the room is dark, quiet, and cool. Think about using blackout curtains, earplugs, or a white noise machine to create a peaceful atmosphere that supports restful sleep.

By prioritizing reliable sleep and considering these practices, you can experience the rejuvenating benefits of quality sleep. I encourage you to reflect on the following questions:

- How can you create a consistent sleep schedule that works for your lifestyle?
- What relaxing activities can you incorporate into your bedtime routine?

- How can you optimize your bedroom environment to promote better sleep?

Remember, sleep is not a luxury but a necessity for your well-being and productivity. Give yourself the gift of reliable sleep and activate your full potential. Put yourself into a sleep state and get as much sleep as possible. Adequate sleep will replenish neurotransmitters that are used for paying attention.

Michael Breus, PhD, the "Sleep Doctor," recommended a five-step plan to optimize your sleep and day when I interviewed him on my podcast *SuccessFULL With ADHD*:

1. Find one wake-up time based on your chronotype. Go to > *chronoquiz.com* to access your chronotype.
2. Stop caffeine by two p.m.
3. Stop alcohol three hours before bed, limiting yourself to two drinks.
4. Exercise daily, and it's usually best to stop four hours before bed.
5. When you wake up in the morning do the "three 15s":
    - Wake up and take fifteen deep breaths.
    - Drink fifteen ounces of water.
    - Go outside and get fifteen minutes of sunlight.

Here are some other recommended resources to help you fall asleep:

- Use the Calm app, Headspace, or Insight Timer to meditate.
- Listen to nature sounds.
- Essential oils.
- Foam roll/massagers.
- Eliminate blue lights from technology used an hour before bed.
- Dim the lights in your house after the sun goes down.

- Take a steam shower under low-lighting conditions.
- Read material you find boring.
- Sleep in cooler temperatures.
- Consider using a noise machine.

Action 9: Stay Accountable

According to the book *Co-Active Coaching* by Henry Kimsey-House, Karen Kimsey-House, Philip Sandahl, and Laura Whitworth, accountability involves the following:

- Knowing WHAT you are going to do.
- Knowing WHEN you will have it done.
- Knowing HOW you will know you did it.

Accountability is a powerful tool that can help us stay on track and achieve our goals. When we hold ourselves accountable, we take ownership of our actions and commit to following through with our commitments.

I have always struggled with maintaining consistency in my work and personal projects. I often started with enthusiasm but would lose motivation along the way, leading to unfinished tasks and unfulfilled goals. I felt frustrated and stuck in a cycle of procrastination.

Recognizing the need for change, I decided to implement accountability measures in my life. I sought out an accountability partner, someone I trust and who shares similar goals and aspirations. Together, we set specific, measurable targets and established regular check-in meetings to review our progress.

By having someone to answer to and share my goals with, I experienced a significant shift in my productivity and commitment. I felt a sense of responsibility to stay true to my word and show up for my accountability partner. The regular check-ins kept me focused, motivated, and on track toward achieving my desired outcomes.

Having an accountability partner has been a game-changer for me. It keeps me motivated, pushes me to overcome obstacles, and ensures that I follow through with my commitments. The sense of accountability has transformed my work ethic and productivity.

To stay accountable and increase your productivity, consider the following strategies:

- Find an Accountability Partner: Seek out a trustworthy individual who shares similar goals or aspirations. Set clear expectations, define your goals, and establish a schedule for regular check-ins or progress updates.

- Set Specific Goals and Deadlines: Clearly define your goals and break them down into actionable steps. Assign deadlines to each task to create a sense of urgency and ensure progress.

- Track Your Progress: Use a tracking system, such as a journal, spreadsheet, or task management app, to monitor your progress. Regularly review and assess your achievements to stay motivated and identify areas for improvement.

By incorporating accountability into my productivity journey, I have created a support system that keeps me focused, motivated, and committed to my goals. I encourage you to embrace the power of accountability and activate your full potential for success. The next section will explore the importance of mindfulness in our productivity journey.

There is something very powerful in your word! Say you are going to do something. Share your goal with a coach, a friend, or loved one. Share it on social media. Identify how you will stay accountable to this goal.

Action 10: Reward Yourself

COACHING ENCOURAGEMENT

We tend to skip this action and move on to the next "thing." I highly encourage you to reward yourself. It doesn't need to be a big reward; it can be a quick five-minute reward.

Rewarding yourself is an essential step in maintaining motivation and celebrating your achievements. When you acknowledge your hard work and treat yourself for reaching milestones, you reinforce positive behaviors and create a sense of fulfillment.

I have always been diligent in my work but struggled with burnout and feeling unappreciated. I realized that I needed to incorporate self-care and rewards into my routine to maintain my motivation and overall well-being. I decided to implement a system of self-rewards for each completed task or milestone achieved.

As I accomplished my goals, I rewarded myself with small treats and activities that brought me joy. It could be anything, but for me it was going out with my friends to a new restaurant, taking time to go out on a boating excursion, or a weekend getaway to the Hamptons or spending quality time with loved ones.

These rewards served as moments of rejuvenation and reminders of my progress.

By integrating self-rewards into my productivity journey, I experienced a renewed sense of motivation and satisfaction. The rewards not only provided much-needed breaks and moments of joy but also reinforced my commitment to achieving my goals.

I used to neglect self-care and forget to celebrate my wins. But incorporating self-rewards has made a significant difference. It reminds me to take care of myself, appreciate my efforts, and stay motivated on my productivity journey.

To effectively reward yourself and boost your productivity, consider the following strategies:

- Define Reward Milestones: Set specific milestones or goals that, when achieved, warrant a reward. It could be completing a challenging project, meeting a deadline, or reaching a significant milestone in your personal or professional life.

- Choose Meaningful Rewards: Select rewards that align with your values and bring you joy. They can be simple, such as indulging in your favorite treat, treating yourself to a spa day, or engaging in a hobby you love.

- Establish a Reward System: Create a system that ensures you follow through with rewarding yourself. It could be a checklist, a reward jar, or a digital tracker. Track your accomplishments and make a conscious effort to celebrate each success.

- Practice Self-Care: Incorporate regular self-care activities into your routine. Take breaks, engage in relaxation techniques, practice mindfulness, or pursue activities that nourish your mind, body, and soul.

By integrating self-rewards into your productivity journey, you create a positive cycle of motivation and self-care. Celebrate your achievements, acknowledge your progress, and prioritize your well-being. Remember, you deserve to be rewarded for your hard work and dedication. Reward yourself for your accomplishments after you take care of your task(s).

Reward Examples:

- Watch your favorite TV show.
- Enjoy a nice bubble bath.
- Play a game.
- Sing a song.
- Throw yourself a dance party.
- Pat yourself on the back.
- Give yourself a high five in the mirror.

Check out >*developgoodhabits.com/reward-yourself/155* for ways to reward yourself.

Summary of the Ten Actions:

1a. Clarify Your To-Dos: Clearly define your to-dos to provide clarity and direction.

1b. Prioritize Your Tasks: Determine your most important tasks and focus on them first.

1c. Schedule Your Day: Create a clear roadmap of tasks and activities to stay focused and on track.

1d. Look at Your Schedule: Regularly review your schedule to be aware of commitments and priorities.

2. Time Yourself: Gain insights into task duration and allocate your time more efficiently.

3. Take Breaks: Rest, recharge, and maintain focus by incorporating regular breaks into your day.

4. Change Your Environment: Optimize your surroundings to enhance focus and productivity.

5. Exercise: Boost energy levels, improve focus, and overall well-being through regular physical activity.

6. Set Your Morning Routine: Establish a purposeful and nourishing routine to start your day.

7. Practice Mindfulness: Embrace mindfulness to reduce stress and cultivate a greater sense of well-being.

8. Get Reliable Sleep: Prioritize quality sleep to rejuvenate and optimize your productivity.

9. Stay Accountable: Hold yourself accountable by seeking support and establishing check-ins.

10. Reward Yourself: Acknowledge your achievements and reinforce positive behaviors through self-rewards.

Your Turn>>

Directions: Answer the questions below.
What was my biggest takeaway from this lesson?

___

___

In the past week or during this lesson, what activities have been energizing, exciting, easier, or peaceful?

___

___

Accountability Questions:

1. *What* small action will I take toward my goals from this lesson?

___

___

2. *When* will I have it done by? (Write a date, day, and time.)

___

___

3. *How* will I know I did it? (What is your measure of knowing that you completed the task?)

___

___

4. *How* will I hold myself accountable or enlist the help of others?

___

___

Extra Space For Your Notes:

STEP 10: PROCRASTINATION

Have you ever thought, "If I didn't do (insert your biggest time waster), I would have been able to accomplish what was important?"

You might even ask yourself, "Where did I spend my time?"

Time. No matter what you do, it keeps on going. The superhero in you likely wants to stop time so you can finish your tasks, get more sleep, exercise, vacation, etc. The one thing you CANNOT buy is time. Think about it: you are using it right now!

What is a time suck? The *Merriam-Webster Dictionary* defines a "time suck" as "an activity to which one devotes a lot of time that might be better or more productively spent doing other things."

Your time suck might be watching TV, listening to a podcast, deep cleaning, organizing, or scrolling through social media. Whatever your answer may be, your answer is what allows you to avoid the intended task.

Here are more examples of time sucks below:

• Transitions • Saying "yes" to too many things • Emails • Phone • Gossiping • Driving • Multitasking • Unnecessary meetings • Disorganization • Wanting "too much" control • Shopping • Time blindness	• Music • Podcasts • Not scheduling your time • Not planning to plan • Not dealing with your anxious thoughts • Hyperfixating on the wrong thing • Looking for lost items • Making too many lists • Snacking/binge eating • Television • Video games • Social media

What are my time sucks?

____

____

____

____

____

When do they usually occur? What time during the day? Is it when I am avoiding something? When I'm tired? When I lack dopamine?

____

____

In order to buy back your time you need to learn how to ***STOP*** sucking your time.

Here are some examples below:

1. Avoid distractions (e.g., phone, computer, or TV) when needing to start a task. Turn off all unnecessary alerts on your phone now!
2. If you do need to use electronics, make it the last thing you do. Block all unnecessary sites by using apps such as Freedom and Forest. If you have an iPhone, you can use the "Focus" feature.
3. If there isn't a show that you really like, turn off the TV.
4. Commit to doing one thing on your list for your optimal focus time. The average optimal focus time is twenty-five minutes (and yours is between ten and forty minutes).
5. Check in with yourself every hour or at scheduled times to make sure you are working toward your goals. (The most successful people do this.)

Next steps:

1. Identify a time during your day when you are late, not getting to the places you want, or completely avoiding a task because of a time suck.
2. How can you avoid this time suck?
3. Commit to avoiding, eliminating, or reducing this time suck when working on a task this week.

Your Turn>>

<u>Directions:</u> Answer the questions below.

What was my biggest takeaway from the time suck lesson?

____

____

In the past week or during this lesson, what activities have been energizing, exciting, easier, or peaceful?

____

____

Accountability Questions:

1. *What* small action will I take toward my goals?

____

____

2. *When* will I have it done by? (Write a date, day, and time.)

____

____

3. *How* will I know I did it? (What is my measure of knowing that I completed the task?)

____

____

4. *How* will I hold myself accountable or enlist the help of others?

Extra Space For Your Notes:

"Either run the day,

or the day will run you."

—Jim Rohn

STEP 11: STOP THE STRESS!

Before reading this book, did you feel like your daily actions and thoughts were constantly in motion like a hamster wheel, not able to stop?

Did you have a hard time hitting the brakes in order to see what was going around you?

A client told me that she felt like a horse in motion with blinders and a carrot attached. She woke up every day continuously on the go, and then some days she couldn't get out of bed. She had no peripheral vision to see beyond her daily tasks and take a look at the whole picture.

Sometimes you have so much chaos going on with your thoughts and physical space that you don't have the capacity to make the space and time to focus on something you truly want. When you are in motion all of the time and not "peripherally" seeing what actions you are taking, it can be hard to see how to sharpen your focus to make real growth. We also don't notice what items are really dragging us down and how to avoid them to clear the chaos in our minds.

Blinded items are items that you are missing or neglecting because of ADHD. Examples include unpaid bills, invoices, outdated designs, guilt, lack of self-care, exercise, frustrations, tasks left uncompleted, text messages owed, donations, doctors' appointments, and unpaid tickets.

Your Turn>>

What are you putting up with? List all of your blinded items:

____

____

____

In order to clear up the space to complete your blinded items and your daily tasks, you are going to learn how to achieve more with less effort.

In this step, you will look at your tasks and organize them to make things a little less daunting and leave you feeling more energized.

STEP 1: List your daily activities in the "Task" column on the next page. This includes personal, academic, professional, and anything in-between.

STEP 2: In the "STOP" column, label your task with an *S*, *T*, *O*, or *P*.

- Use *S* for activities that **STRESS** you.
- Use *T* for activities that are **TIME-CONSUMING**.
- Use *O* for activities that are **ORDINARY.**
- Use *P* for activities that feel **POWERFUL**.

STEP 3: How many hours a week do you spend on each task? Put that information in the "Hours a week" column.

Task	STOP	Hours a week

STEP 4: Transfer your weekly tasks into each quadrant below.

(S)tressed	(T)ime-Consuming
(O)rdinary	**(P)owerful**

Many of us spend most of our time on big project tasks. But what could you focus on and let go of that would add to your productivity? Use your task list to answer the questions below:

1. Where do I spend most of my time? (Write down what percent of the time you spend on each task.)

____

____

2. Can I break down any of the *T* tasks into smaller ones?

____

____

3. Are there any *S* tasks I can delegate, eliminate, or push off?

____

____

4. Can any of my *S* tasks be done during a session with a body double or can it be done after I perform a *P* task?

____

____

Now, why not commit to putting your tasks somewhere obvious—so you can refer to them as the week progresses?

I will put my tasks (name the location below; for example, a coffee table, my desk, in my planner): _______________________________

Directions: Answer the questions below.

What was my biggest takeaway from the STOP lesson?

____

____

In the past week or during this lesson, what activities have been energizing, exciting, easier, or peaceful?

____

____

Accountability Questions:

1. *What* small action will I take toward my goals? (Note: it could be what you listed as your blinded item.)

____

____

2. *When* will I have it done by? (Write a date, day, and time.)

____

____

3. *How* will I know I did it? (What is your measure of knowing that you completed the task?)

____

____

4. *How* will I hold myself accountable or enlist the help of others?

____

____

Extra Space For Your Notes:

"Ask for help. Not because you are weak.

But because you want to remain strong."

—Les Brown

STEP 12: NEXT-LEVEL REQUESTS TO FEEL EMPOWERED

Do you experience people-pleasing tendencies?

Do you care more about what other people think about you and often don't share what you really want or feel until you finally break down or explode?

Many individuals with ADHD are people-pleasers and do not like asking for help. An option is to delegate. I am sure this must be a little uneasy for you, especially if you are not used to doing it or have not previously had the tools.

But now you have momentum! If you've been doing these tasks, you are more productive and confident in your tasks and goals. You are more confident in yourself!

Now you need a further challenge. This is usually the section that people try to avoid!

I challenge you to do this activity; speak with your accountability partner and challenge yourself to complete this section! It will likely be uneasy for you—even scary—but I promise you will feel alive and more empowered after it is completed.

In this section, I will ask you to commit to a challenge.

"A challenge is a request designed to have you move to the outer limits of what you feel is possible. Challenges are much bigger than a request and will typically take your breath away. The end result is that you will generally stretch further from where you were originally, and may even take on more of a task than what was requested."

—Jennifer Britton

Here are two types of challenges that you can do:

Option # 1: Make a bold request or have a difficult conversation with someone you've been avoiding.

Option # 2: Ask someone to do something for you that you normally would do for another person.

If you chose option # 1, I have laid out some framework below to help you with a difficult conversation.

A. Think about the main reason you are avoiding this conversation (make this your starter).

For example: *"I have been avoiding having this conversation because I have been fearing that you would get upset and not share your honest thoughts with me in the future."*

Your Turn>>

____

____

____

B. Seek to understand instead of pushing your agenda and forcing them to understand.

For example: *"So the other day you came home and I had dinner ready, you saw it and said, "I thought we were having Italian tonight?"*

Your Turn>>

____

____

____

C. Discuss the impact of not understanding. *Make sure to use "I" statements here.

For example: *"My first thought was that you didn't appreciate the work I put into making Mexican food, but then I gave it more thought. Perhaps I took it the wrong way?"*

Your Turn>>

____

____

____

D. Work TOGETHER to problem-solve and create a solution.

For example: *"So can you help me understand? I really want to understand what you meant by that."*

Your Turn>>

Now, LISTEN to the person's response and do not push your answer.

See if you can come to some sort of mutual understanding. Things to think about from here:

- Try not to get caught up in how you feel. Try to listen to what the other person is saying and see it from their perspective as they're sharing it with you.
- If things aren't going according to plan, take a break or agree to disagree.

Now put it all together below:

Your Turn>>

Consider practicing this in the mirror or with someone else before having the conversation. It is best to have the actual conversation in person if you can, or by phone, not over text.

If you chose option #2, some examples of bold requests would be something out of the ordinary that you wouldn't typically ask from someone else. Others may very well ask you to do this, and you would likely do it, but generally speaking, you would not ask others for this.

Ideas:

- Ask someone who is going to the dry cleaners to take your laundry with them.
- Ask someone who is grocery shopping if they can get you some items that you need.
- Request an award or a scholarship.
- Ask for an article to be published.
- Ask a mentor to mentor you.

The bold request *may or may not* be answered with a "yes." However, the sheer act of the request will further empower you!

Your Turn>>

What was my biggest takeaway from the next-level request lesson?

____

____

In the past week or during this lesson, what activities have been energizing, exciting, easier, or peaceful?

____

____

Accountability Questions:

1. *What* small action will I take toward my goals?

____

____

2. *When* will I have it done by? (Write a date, day, and time.)

____

____

3. *How* will I know I did it? (What is your measure of knowing that you completed the task?)

____

____

4. *How* will I hold myself accountable or enlist the help of others?

____

____

Extra Space For Your Notes:

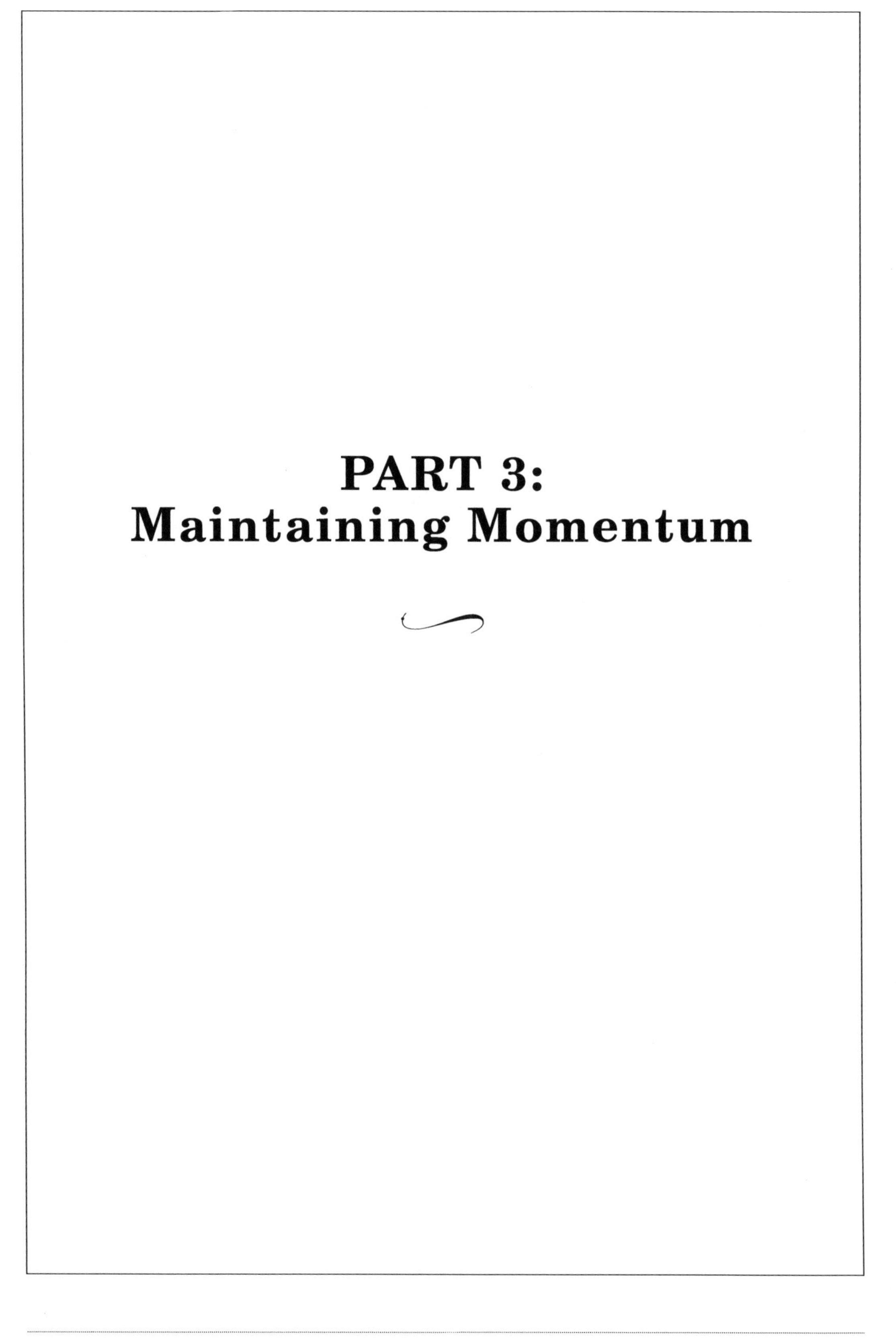

PART 3: Maintaining Momentum

"REFLECTION. Looking back so that the view looking forward is even clearer."

—Unknown

CHAPTER 5

I Have Built Momentum. Now What?

Before we move on we need to reflect. Please answer the questions below before we figure out what your next step is:

What have I learned from *Activate Your ADHD Potential: A 12-Step Journey from Chaos to Confidence for Adults with ADHD*?

____

____

What will I take away in terms of learning (i.e., new perspectives, insights, etc.)?

____

____

Reflect upon the learning journey (i.e., difficult, easy, different, rewarding, etc.).

____

____

What were the last twelve steps like for me?

____

____

What were my biggest takeaways?

____

____

How will I apply my new learning to my daily life at work, school, and/or at home?

____

____

Great! Now we can move on to the next step!

If you skipped the past few questions (as I'm sure most of us will), please consider going back and completing them. They will help you in reflecting on your journey and the hard work you have committed to over the course of the past twelve steps.

As an individual with ADHD, I know this can be very hard as we constantly want to move on to the next step without reflecting on what we have accomplished. But hopefully, with the tools that you have utilized in this book, you can continue to stop and reflect on your accomplishments and acknowledge them before moving on to the next thing. This will help you truly understand what you have accomplished and focus less on the gap and more on the gain!

Do you need to go back to the previous questions? If so, please take five to ten minutes or as much time as you need to complete these before moving on to this section.

What's Next?

In this section, we wrap up the potential paths you might want to take to continue your personal development journey. There are many different ways, and some are listed here to help guide you on your own path. Please review this chapter after going through Chapter 4. Otherwise, this chapter will not make sense to you.

Hopefully, by now you have spent the past twelve weeks (if you did it faster or slower, it's not a problem—we all move at our own pace) working through CWB's 12-Step Journey to gain greater confidence!

What was the biggest takeaway that you got out of finishing this book? How did it feel to slow down the chaos and spend time working on yourself?

If you used the CWB Accountability Group, what did you think of being held accountable?

Did you feel like accountability helped you in achieving your goals?

Hopefully, by now you feel you have more space to maintain momentum. Since we are lifelong learners, it is important to continue to create goals for yourself so you build more traction and maintain momentum.

What are your goals for the next three months? Feel free to create new goals for yourself using your mind map lesson first. Then follow it with steps three, six, seven, and eleven. Remember to make sure that you always incorporate your values and strengths (steps four and five) into your goals in addition to making sure your dopamine levels are as regulated as they can be (step eight). You do not need to redo steps one, four, five, eight, nine, and twelve as you create new goals. However, you should keep notice of the principles behind them as you take action on your new goals.

Feel free to get access to these blank worksheets using the link here > *bit.ly/CWBworksheets*

"One way to keep momentum going is to have constantly greater goals."

—Michael Korda

CHAPTER 6

The Secret Support System That Maintains Momentum

You were taught this support system as a kid, but everyone overlooked it. We were accountable to our parents and teachers when we were children. Hopefully, in the CWB process, you have maximized your executive functions to work more independently toward reaching your goals.

Although ADHDers hate structure, we thrive off it at the same time. In order to maintain momentum, we need some level of structure and ongoing accountability. This might be through your partner, your friends, social media, reminders, a coach, or even a group.

You have five options when it comes to support.

Option #1: You can do nothing. But why would you want to do nothing? You just spent hard work and time working on YOU and improving your quality of life and the chaos of your ADHD. The wonderful thing about our brains is that neuroplasticity helps to rewire our neurons. The bad thing about our brains is that it atrophies when we don't continue practicing what we've learned. I'm sure you're thinking, "Really? I just spent all this time. I thought this was it!" The tools you have learned in this book are fundamental to your new life and awareness of your ADHD brain, but you need continued practice to continue to grow.

Option #2: Use the downloads from my website to continue your journey. Start or continue using our CWB Adult ADHD Support Group for body doubling, support, and accountability with like-minded individuals. While doing this you can go back and print out the worksheets and create goals for yourself using the system *Activate Your ADHD Potential: A 12-Step Journey from Chaos to Confidence for Adults with ADHD > bit.ly/ChaosToConfidence* and work at your own pace.

Option #3: Join our Activated With ADHD Group for adults eighteen and older with ADHD. This is a low-cost option to continue to receive weekly support from our amazing CWB Coaches, new lessons, group coaching, and opportunities to schedule body doubling.

Here is some feedback from this group:

"It was a fantastic session! Super glad I signed up."

"I am excited and hopeful!"

"Never in my life have I felt like I 'belonged' during a group coaching/therapy session!"

"Even though the ADHD has been a toughie, I managed to write two Amazon best-selling books during the pandemic. I've never experienced a small group like yours. I'm equipped better than I was and that's to be celebrated! I'm brilliant!"

"Thx for posting about the app 'Endel.' I go to sleep like a baby nightly. I listen to it several times a day to de-stress. Game-changer. I also set my office up in a way that is less stressful. I asked a component of what I needed at my job … I now work from home more … in my office. Win-win! Thank you for impacting my life virtually and on IG! Several wins!"

Option #4: I have created a continuation group for my clients called Maintaining Momentum™. Maintaining Momentum™ is a small group that helps you feel supported and accountable and leads you to reach new levels of success through bigger and better goals and visions.

Check out Sav's journey:

"I'm so glad I found Brooke! The group calls really transformed my life this season.

I think for the first time ever I don't feel alone or defeated because of my ADHD struggles. I feel empowered to try things differently and honor the way my mind works instead of condemning it. I'll be recommending Coaching With Brooke to all my friends and colleagues with ADHD!"—Sav, photographer, Tennessee

If you are interested in joining this group, please feel free to check out the link > *coachingwithbrooke.com/maintainingmomentum* to learn more and register.

Option #5: If you are looking for more customized support from one of our coaches, you might want to consider individual adult, student, and parent coaching that can be found here. Visit > *coachingwithbrooke.com* to learn more and register.

Check out some of the reviews from our previous clients:

"Working with Brooke was a great experience. She really helped me change fundamental processes in my business and mindset that help me work more efficiently and more productively. Having a coach by my side so I could work through pain points and be held accountable has been transformative for my business and has also translated to all parts of my life."—Beatriz, entrepreneur interior designer, Boca Raton, Florida

"I was getting burned out after working with students pretty much all my life! I hired Brooke to revive my heart, mind, and spirit ... and boy did she ever! I am happier, more organized, and even have more time for my hockey leagues, skating, skiing, lifting travel, and all the sports I so love to do! Brooke is a miracle worker, and she has most definitely lifted some huge weights off my shoulders. My tutoring business is running more efficiently and effectively because of Coaching With Brooke!!!"—Karen, owner of tutoring business, Naples, Florida

"Working with Brooke has single-handedly changed my professional AND personal life. The tools I learned from her have already evolved my organizational, self-care, and business management skills. I would refer Brooke to everyone I know! Whether you are looking for support in your business or trying to work through personal issues, Brooke is your person. She is kind, comprehensive, professional, and brilliant."—Missy, singer, comedian, creative agency entrepreneur, New York City

"Trust begins with yourself,

Trust yourself first and you will

start trusting others in life."

—Invajy

CHAPTER 7

Client Experiences with CWB's 12-Step Journey—This Really Works!

Before we wrap up this workbook, I want you to be encouraged by a few stories of clients who have been transformed through Coaching With Brooke by implementing the strategies in this workbook and by our coaching team.

Client #1—Diane: COO and Wife

COACHING ENCOURAGEMENT

This chapter is meant to inspire you and connect with the struggles and successes of other clients like you. If the successes of these clients are triggering you due to your perceived failures, do not worry. Feel free to skip this chapter.

Diane came to me in 2022. She is a professional with ADHD who has done a lot of professional development. Diane has a great marriage and is the first person in her family to create wealth and graduate from college.

Identifying your disruptors is so important. She came to me and said, "Brooke,

I am overwhelmed."

We did a coaching deep dive and realized that she wasn't overwhelmed. She was underwhelmed.

Diane was stuck in the monotony of the same tasks and roles, none of which brought her joy. She had a boss who micromanaged her. She knew her strengths and weaknesses, but she didn't tap into them. After she ascended to a senior level position at her company, her employer recommended that she hire a coach to help with her "productivity."

Diane and I worked together for three months. We addressed the obstacles that kept her from activating her true potential:

- Her boss's micromanagement
- Family that overwhelmed her
- Underwhelm in her life when it came to starting a family

Diane evaluated different areas of her life. She wanted to focus on her career and find systems of organization that worked for her. She felt that without them she would be buried. She believed that systems that worked for her would demonstrate a new Diane to others. She knew she needed them to keep her from falling behind and promising but not delivering. Her finances were a source of shame. She was in debt and wanted to pay down her credit card. She wanted to meet fitness and nutrition goals.

In my first coaching session with Diane, we uncovered how sleep issues negatively impacted her mornings. We worked on slow rolling her morning, a method where a person takes their time to get settled in the morning before starting the workday.

Before we met, Diane had already done the work on understanding her strengths and values. This allowed us to quickly create a daily schedule that had start and end times for her work tasks. We set up an accountability meeting with one of her co-workers to make sure that Diane did the following:

- Spend two hours each week on busywork
- Spend time working from home so she could complete unfinished work from her scheduled times

When she followed her schedule, there were times that she had to stop in the middle of an uncompleted task to go on to her next task.

In the next few sessions, we worked on discerning when to say "no" to additional responsibilities. We tackled how to prioritize a to-do list.

Diane started noticing how "planning to plan" changed her life. When she didn't plan, things got hectic. The initial schedule we created needed to be tweaked, so we adjusted as Diane grew in her confidence and momentum. She also grew in delegation, which allowed her to focus on what was important to her.

Once Diane controlled the chaos of her schedule and to-dos, she realized that her job was not something she truly wanted to do. She learned that she had been giving away her power because she often viewed what she did as inferior and not good enough. The micromanaging and controlling role was not for her. Although the job aligned with her strengths, there were too many restrictions for her to feel truly happy and passionate about her daily life.

We started to work on Diane's bigger picture. We couldn't do that until she had the space to think about what is truly important to her. I started asking Diane, "Considering your strengths, values, and passions, what would be motivating to you?"

Diane felt that in order to create the space she needed to answer that question, she needed to quit her job. She gave her boss notice that by the end of 2022, she would leave. I know that many people would think, "How can you quit if you don't have another job already?" Diane and I worked on her finances so that she would pay down debt and have enough saved in case she didn't work for many months. This would give her the freedom to passionately work on herself.

Diane had fertility issues and struggled to conceive. Shortly after she gave her boss notice, she became pregnant.

Diane is a great example of someone who was healed of the lie that she was not good enough. She was no longer obsessed with her physical appearance. She created the space to discover what truly made her happy and passionate in life.

Client #2—Megan: A Late-Twenties Entrepreneur and Online Coach

Megan originally came to Coaching With Brooke to gain awareness of her ADHD symptoms. She wanted to be off medication and more effectively manage her ADHD. She wanted to start an online business but didn't know where to start.

She constantly compared herself to others and wanted to "keep up with the

Joneses." She never thought she was enough. She felt she didn't do enough for her morning routine. She felt inferior to her neurotypical brother. She felt compelled to be the best in her industry, but she didn't have ENOUGH followers or cutting-edge programs.

Megan and I worked together in an individualized setting for two months. In the first month, she tripled her online income. Despite this initial success, Megan was still overwhelmed with where to focus her energy. She was constantly disrupted by comparisons.

Diane, the first client, spent a lot of time on values and strengths before we met. Megan had not done this, so we worked to clarify her values, goals, strengths, and motivations. She thought that success required a structured morning routine that included reading. Megan learned that while these are good things, they aren't necessary. Sometimes coaching involves leading people away from the presuppositions that chain them down.

We worked on what worked for her unique ADHD brain. I learned that Megan was having difficulty falling asleep and waking up without the use of technology. She dragged throughout each day. Her boyfriend went to bed later than her, so Megan felt she needed to stay up. She defaulted to mindless time on her phone to keep herself awake.

We planned a way for her to go to sleep earlier. We devised ways for her to not look at her phone, but still use it if necessary before bed. For example, she would put on her Bluetooth headphones so she could listen to a book or meditation app, but she needed to leave her phone on the opposite side of her room so she didn't pick it up. She would use her phone as an alarm clock but installed apps that prevented her from using her phone first thing in the morning. She created space to spend time on herself in the morning.

Once we created that space, we worked on how she would fill the time.

- She left her planner on her coffee table downstairs. When she went downstairs in the morning she would be reminded of it. Individuals with ADHD very often have working memory issues and forget to do something if they don't see it.

- When she passed by her planner she would make coffee and sit on her couch, where she would review what she had coming up for the day and reflect on the previous day.

- On some days, she took a walk to increase her dopamine levels.
- After a few months, she added stimulants to her morning routine which helped her manage ADHD, dopamine, and anxiety.

This plan relaxed her and decreased stress about what she should do in the morning.

After one month, we continued to work together one-on-one and decided that Megan would join one of our groups. We continued this path for three months. In the group setting, Megan felt more confident in her abilities to be a leading expert in her field and a confident entrepreneur. She also felt happier and more supportive of her partner. Megan was more comfortable in her own skin and abilities. We implemented more time management strategies. We discussed how to have uncomfortable conversations she'd been avoiding. Together we mapped out her goals and future desires.

After those initial four months, Megan joined Coaching With Brooke's Maintaining Momentum™ group where she continued to be accountable while using the tools she had learned in our individual and group coaching sessions.

The turning point for Megan was when she used the Why Funnel. This clarified her motivations, released a lot of the "shoulds," and focused her goals. After one year of working together, Megan no longer needed our services. She was thriving in life and business. She now uses the Why Funnel in her own coaching practice. Megan has referred many clients to us. They are ADHDers who were amazed at Megan's quick success and wanted to grow as she had.

Client #3—Tedd: Thirty-Eight-Year-Old Businessman

Tedd came to Coaching With Brooke as a single man who was depressed, anxious, and extremely overwhelmed with his work role. Tedd couldn't focus on any real-life priorities.

He wanted to work on his career, purpose, health and fitness, and personal growth. When he started he ranked having a significant other and romance as a zero out of ten in his life. At first, he didn't want to focus on that aspect of life.

In our first session, Tedd said he was experiencing overwhelm with everything going on and the changes at work. He started off by completing the life cups, strengths, and values lessons. Motivated to make a change, he mind mapped what he wanted to create in his job. Determined to find a new role, he completed the

STOP time management exercise to discover what stressed him. We learned he did not like completing a lot of tasks throughout the day, managing others at work, attending meetings, or multitasking. However, this was basically his job description.

Clarity came to Tedd about his values, strengths, stresses, and energizers. He decided that he needed to exercise to manage his anxiety, stay focused, and take off some of the stress from his demanding job. We set a goal for him to exercise with a trainer three times a week. He liked working with a trainer for intense workouts and accountability. When we reviewed his goal of personal growth, we decided that Tedd needed to make time for things he enjoyed.

Just like Tedd needed a personal trainer to push his workouts, Tedd decided that he needed to join our accountability and support group, Maintaining Momentum™. This added a layer of accountability and awareness for him at the very beginning of our journey together.

Starting in our second session, we worked on Tedd's morning routine, mindfulness, nutrition, supplements, and sleep. Tedd walked away with these key insights:

- Less is more.
- It doesn't have to be perfect.
- Start with YOU before moving on to everything else during the day.
- Breaks are NECESSARY.

Tedd next completed his Why Funnel to discover his motivation for his three goals. Tedd worked on these goals for several weeks with the accountability of the group. We then reviewed values three weeks later. Tedd learned that he tended to overcommit, compared himself to others, and lived with an all-or-nothing mentality.

Tedd also learned the negative impact these made in his life. He acknowledged the burnout. He made changes. He declared that the grass was not always greener on the other side. He started taking days for himself.

In our remaining one-on-one sessions, we worked on reframing his negative unintentional thoughts through some CBT-like exercises. I led Tedd in writing his story on a piece of paper and how to differentiate between facts and fiction, because he created many stories about himself that were far from the truth. We addressed how to calm his central nervous system by meditating on his thoughts using meditation apps.

Tedd mapped out small time slots in his day for himself. This included time for exercise, coaching, time to "be," sleep, waking up, and morning routine. To be accountable, he sent me his daily schedule with his tasks for himself and his work.

In our final individual coaching session, Tedd had several breakthrough discoveries:

- His happiness was more important than the money he made.
- His "all-or-nothing" approach was absolutely unsustainable.
- He needed to focus on one thing at a time.
- He wasn't successfully delegating.
- He wasn't 100% sure what to delegate.
- He was too often saying "yes" to other people.

At our last one-on-one session, Tedd and I scheduled his next three months and prioritized his actions and goals in his new calendar system. He would finish the CWB's 12-Week Process outside of our individual coaching session and continued to seek support and accountability through Maintaining Momentum™ for the next two years.

Within two months of our individual coaching journey, the desire for romance went from zero out of ten to ten out of ten. He found his soon-to-be wife. He proposed to her several weeks after meeting her, and they are still together.

He started therapy again, worked on disordered eating, and moved. He took a class that led him to a new career path. He graduated at the top of his class. He still works at the same company, but he has spoken up on his own behalf. He asked management to delegate some of his responsibilities to new employees. He expressed his desire to manage less. Although his current career is not his lifelong dream, he has mapped out more of what he enjoys doing and has created space for himself, his wife, and his new life.

Client #4—Joey: Nineteen-Year-Old College Freshman

Joey came to me as a freshman in college after failing out of his first semester with a 1.9 GPA. In high school, he was an honors student, well-liked, a teacher's pet, captain of his sports team, and the guy who everyone wanted to be around. He fell apart in his first semester at college. He did not have the executive function skills to keep up his grades and thrive. Teachers and parents had given him structure in high school. He realized he no longer had that in college. Joey knew that he needed to get coaching, and his family supported him in this.

In our first session, we dove into what wasn't working and where he wanted to focus. Academics was first. Other areas of focus were health, fitness, and creating time to visit his family back home. They were close and he valued their time together.

We discussed his motivation for these goals using the Why Funnel. Joey and I took a deep dive into his daily activities and classes. The study methods he used in high school weren't working in college. We determined his optimal focus time and when he should study. We talked through how to increase dopamine and gain focus from his workouts. He was determined to get out of his dorm room more. Once we built an accountability system and schedule around these items, he boosted his GPA to 3.8 in his second semester. Joey was highly motivated and transformed his education in one month through scheduling and accountability.

Joey and I worked together for four months because he wanted accountability and momentum help during that second semester. He continued the momentum without my help by continuing the positive habits we worked on together and by enlisting his friends, family, and professors in his accountability for success. From time to time, we would meet when new obstacles came into his life—like the COVID lockdown. In the end, he graduated with high honors and is thriving as a young adult.

Testimonies about CWB

"I was first recommended to Brooke by an ADHD nutrition coach that I love. My nutrition coach said Brooke was amazing and her work was exceptional. After meeting with Brooke multiple times, I'm having a hard time figuring out what word I should add after 'exceptional.' That's Brooke. She is intelligent, driven, insightful, and passionate about helping others. Her impressive background in education gives her a unique perspective and skill. Her neurodiverse mind and entrepreneurial experience elevate that skill set to the next level. Brooke has built a team of professionals to help you activate your potential regardless of your stage of life or goals. I cannot recommend her highly enough. I have no doubt this is only the beginning for both her and the Coaching With Brooke team."—Gwen, ADHD thought leader

"I met with Brooke virtually in 2019. Years later I am still using the skills gained from our sessions on a daily basis. I did not recognize my ADHD until I was an adult, so when I first connected with Brooke, I was struggling professionally. I still use her resources in my professional and personal life years later. Thank you, Brooke!"—Amy, entrepreneur

"I found Brooke on Instagram and she has changed my life over the last year and a half. Last year I was diagnosed with ADHD and immediately felt like my world was coming down around me. Brooke and her team helped me make sense of it all. Now I'm living a much more structured and informed ADHD life! I did her 3C Activation© and twelve-week course and continued working with her in the Maintaining Momentum group.—Haley, registered dietitian

"It's hard to overstate the impact Brooke had on my life. She might specialize in coaching professionals with ADHD, but honestly, she's the best career coach I've ever had, regardless of my ADHD.

"I found Brooke at the same time I was at a crossroads in a major career decision. I'm deeply grateful for her sage advice. After years as a high-functioning nonprofit executive, I hit a jarring roadblock, and it became clear to me that navigating around it (or plowing through it!) meant finally understanding the adult ADHD diagnosis I received (and ignored) six years ago. Before I could make a major choice about my next career steps, I needed to fully understand my neurodivergent brain and take back my power by harnessing my strengths rather than sinking into what I believed were my lifelong weaknesses. Brooke gave me the tools to harness the good parts of ADHD and to put guardrails up against the challenging parts. It wasn't until I did the work on myself that I could work through the larger question about my career path, which Brooke once again deftly helped me navigate. A five-star review feels so small compared to how much she did for me. I could not recommend her more and will forever be indebted to her."—Rachel, nonprofit C-level executive

"Coaching With Brooke has changed my life! Brooke is knowledgeable, resourceful, insightful, kind, and compassionate. She really cares and there are really no words to describe how great she is! I am very grateful for her guidance! Coach Brooke truly deserves ten stars!"—Nancy, real estate lawyer

"I have known Brooke personally for twenty years, and I have been working with her for the last four years. She is a godsend. Our weekly group sessions are exactly what I need since I work alone at home. If you are an adult and have ADHD, she will save your life."—Peter, photographer

"I have to give this service five stars. For people looking for direction and to make sense of their ADHD and their lives, I've found Coaching With Brooke to be a vital and richly rewarding resource. You can go for the one-on-one option. I did that and found the coaches to be insightful, wise, and kind. You can also opt for group sessions, which rewarded me in a slightly different way. It's reassuring to know that there is no shortage of people like me who also seek direction on how to navigate living with a brain that likes to zig when I need to zag. I unconditionally recommend Coaching With Brooke, and I've found it to be a stellar investment. Five stars!"—Michael, journalist and former professional boxer

"10/10 recommend! *I love how I feel and how I know that I have seen* ***growth*** *during my time with coaching. Before coaching, I learned about why my brain is the way it is, but I was missing the* ***accountability*** *and* ***support*** *I needed. My coach has been so* ***supportive*** *and* ***encouraging****. I used to feel like a failure on a regular basis, but now I know I can live a life being* ***resilient*** *and* ***successful****."*—Zoë, student and ADHD advocate

"I reached out to Brooke for help after an absolutely brutal first semester in college. With my combination of ADHD, poor time management skills, and a bogus organizational system, I hit rock bottom and was told I would be asked to leave my honors program at school if I didn't get my act together. Brooke continuously helped me by brainstorming some unique strategies that would help me focus on my work and keep me accountable for the daily and long-term goals we had set. I met with her once a week for long meetings but could text her whenever I had an issue. She responded super quickly with helpful tips. She's crazily organized and helped me turn my grades around and improve in other areas. I could not recommend her enough. 6/5 stars."—Christian, college student

"I hadn't realized just how serious ADHD can be! You hear of it all the time and blow it off. You think a child is hyper and give him a pill. Parents, that's not the case. ADHD is a serious condition that needs to be managed. If you want your child to succeed at school, and in life, they have to learn how to manage their personal

effects from ADHD. As parents, it is our job to provide every tool to make our children productive in the real world. No one can do it alone. As they say, 'It takes a village.' I took on the role of the team leader to get everyone in place as my son was approaching sixth grade. Thanks to Brooke and her team I am proud to say that after a long year of learning lessons and working diligently, our son made the honor roll. We can never thank Brooke enough for her absolute dedication, knowledge, and attention to detail."—Abbey, parent of a twelve-year-old son with ADHD

"I joined a 3C Activation Coaching group (twelve weeks) upon my later-in-life diagnosis, a group led by coach Brooke. In terms of daily functionality, emotional regulation, and self-awareness, it was an enormous game-changer. It provided exercises that continue to steer me toward communications and actions which are aligned with my strengths and values. At fifty-four, I am finally at the helm of my life with a healthy understanding of how I got here, how I operate in default mode, and how I can now channel my energy in more positive manners."—Michael, chef and lawyer, Boca Raton, Florida

"I've been looking for Coaching With Brooke my whole life, I found my tribe. I have always known I had something that would hold me back and couldn't describe. I figured I was making stuff up in my head or excusing it as if I didn't have the ability to succeed in the basics of life. When discovering that there is a way to understand our unique ADHD brains, it all becomes clear. The practice and knowledge you get from Brooke's way of overcoming our struggles helps you achieve your own personal and career goals. ***I promise you that if you jump on board with Brooke's program, you will feel empowered to overcome any struggles that could be holding you back."***—Priscilla, manager at Apple, Orlando, Florida

“You’re Never Over.”

—Eminem

THE SECRET CHAPTER

Is This Book *Really* Done Already?

You know when you get to the end of a really good television series and you are sad and depressed, not knowing what to do next?

In case you feel that way about this book, I have copied the links to some recommendations below that you can reference, because you and I both know that self-development is never done!

CWB Tried-and-True Recommendations

EDUCATION:

ADHD Experts:

- Edward M. Hallowell, MD
- Daniel G. Amen, MD
- Thomas E. Brown, PhD
- John J. Ratey, MD
- Russell Barkley, PhD
- Russell Ramsay, PhD

Brooke's ADHD Book List:

- *ADHD 2.0* by Edward M. Hallowell, MD, and John J. Ratey, MD
- *Healing ADD* by Daniel G. Amen, MD
- *Driven to Distraction* by Edward M. Hallowell, MD, and John J. Ratey, MD
- *Attention Deficit Disorder* by Thomas E. Brown, PhD
- *Smart But Stuck* by Thomas E. Brown, PhD
- *When an Adult You Love Has ADHD* by Russell Barkley, PhD
- *The ADHD Effect on Marriage* by Melissa Orlov
- *What Your ADHD Child Wishes You Knew: Working Together to Empower Kids for Success in School and Life* by Sharon Saline, PsyD
- *8 Keys to Parenting Children with ADHD* by Cindy Goldrich, EdM, ADHD-CCSP

Brooke's Self-Development and Mindset Book List:

- *Limitless* by Jim Kwik
- *The One Thing* by Gary Keller and Jay Papasan
- *The Power of When: Discover Your Chronotype—and the Best Time to Eat Lunch, Ask for a Raise, Have Sex, Write a Novel, Take Your Meds, and More* by Michael Breus, PhD
- *Eat That Frog!* by Brian Tracy
- *The Miracle Morning* by Hal Elrod
- *Managing Oneself* by Peter Drucker
- *Self Coaching 101* by Brooke Castillo
- *Atomic Habits* by James Clear
- *The 7 Habits of Highly Effective People* by Stephen R. Covey
- *The Science of Stuck* by Britt Frank and Sasha Heinz

Podcasts/Webisodes:

- *ADHD Power Tools* with Brooke Schnittman and Ali Idriss
- *SuccessFULL With ADHD* with Brooke Schnittman

SUPPORT:

ADHD and Binge Eating Specialists:

- Becca King @adhd.nutritionist
- Nicole DeMasi Malcher @eatingwithADHD
- Brittany Modell @nofoodfears
- Marissa Kai Miluk @binge.nutritionist

Couples Coaching:

- Melissa Orlov

Community/Accountability & Connection:

- CWB Adult ADHD Facebook Support Group (clients and alumni only)
- CWB Body Doubling Group (clients and alumni only)
- Coaching With Brooke Instagram and Facebook: @coachingwithbrooke

ADHD Support Groups

- CHADD
- ADDA
- ACO
- *ADDitude* magazine
- Renafi
- Activated With ADHD

Planners:

- Passion Planner (go to > bit.ly/ChaosToConfidence for coupon code)
- Bullet Journal
- Planner Pad

Focusing Hacks:

- Centerpointe.com
- Time Timer
- Pomodoro Apps
- Loop Ear Plugs (go to > bit.ly/ChaosToConfidence for coupon code)
- Yogi fidget toy (go to > bit.ly/ChaosToConfidence for coupon code)
- Noisli (go to > bit.ly/ChaosToConfidence for coupon code)

Organization Tools:

- Find out what type of organization style you have and how to organize at Clutterbug.me
- *Organizing Solutions for People with ADHD* by Susan Pinsky
- ADHD Power Tools-Episode 44-Organization and Episode 52-Organization 2 > *bit.ly/ADHDPOWERTOOLS*

Which tools will I take away from this chapter?

____

____

What is my plan after reading this book?

A. Am I going to check out some of the recommendations in this secret chapter? If yes, then what?

____

____

B. Am I going to consider following one of the recommendations in chapter six?

____

____

If you need a reminder, here they are:

1. Free Option: Do nothing

2. Free Option: Downloads > *bit.ly/ChaosToConfidence* — continue to participate in the CWB Adult ADHD Discord Community here > *bit.ly/CWBDiscord*

3. Low-Cost Option: Activated with ADHD—Adult ADHD Membership: > *coachingwithbrooke.com/activated*

4. Mid-Cost Option: Maintaining Momentum—Adult ADHD Group Coaching: > *coachingwithbrooke.com/maintainingmomentum*

5. Higher-Cost Option: Individual coaching with a CWB coach: > *coachingwithbrooke.com/letusshowyouhow*

ABOUT THE AUTHOR

Brooke Schnittman, MA, PCC, BCC, is a compassionate ADHD coach who has worked alongside ADHDers and their families since 2006. Ironically, Brooke was diagnosed with ADHD in 2019. Her personal experiences with ADHD in her own life, her family life, and her professional life have given her a deep understanding of how ADHD can impact an individual's education, psyche, relationships, and career.

Brooke earned a bachelor's degree in education from Penn State in 2006 and a master's degree in special education from New York University in 2007. Brooke worked with ADHDers in the school system until 2018.

Upon leaving public education, Brooke created the 3C Activation© program, which has changed the lives of thousands of adults with ADHD by creating new awareness and understanding of their ADHD brains and how to work with them rather than against them. The 3C Activation© program has helped some of her clients multiply their income, heal relationships, create balance and joy, improve communication, increase business productivity, organize home and work, and complete tasks they have started.

Brooke has built a team of ADHD coaches at Coaching With Brooke LLC, which offers coaching and resources to over one million individuals with ADHD daily and aims to impact 100 million over the next five years.

Brooke has paved the way to spread ADHD awareness and tools by creating the first-ever ADHD EdCamp in 2020. Thousands of worldwide attendees have been able to attend this free camp and connect with hundreds of ADHD experts.

She is one of the leading ADHD sources on Instagram. You can find her personal and coaching ADHD journey featured in magazines and websites such as *Forbes*, *Entrepreneur*, *ADDitude*, and CHADD. Her work has also been featured on news outlets such as CBS, NBC, and FOX. She is a keynote international speaker and has given workshops for Chopra Global, the International ADHD Conference, the Event Planner Expo, and more. Her leading podcast, *SuccessFULL With ADHD*, is a resource where you can gain tips for breaking free from the disruption cycles. On her podcast, Brooke chats with ADHDers with success stories, celebrity ADHDers, and the foremost ADHD experts (such as Edward M. Hallowell, MD, Daniel G. Amen, MD, and Gabor Maté, MD).

@Coachingwithbrooke on Instagram and Facebook

Made in the USA
Las Vegas, NV
23 November 2023